Whispers of a Savage Sort

Also by the author

Men with Their Hands: A Novel

Assembly Required: Notes from a Deaf Gay Life

Snooty: A Comedy

This Way to the Acorns: Poems

Silence Is a Four-Letter Word: On Art & Deafness

St. Michael's Fall: Poems

As Editor

Eyes of Desire 2: A Deaf GLBT Reader

When I Am Dead: The Writings of George M. Teegarden

Eyes of Desire: A Deaf Gay & Lesbian Reader

www.raymondluczak.com

Whispers of a Savage Sort
And Other Plays about the Deaf American Experience

Raymond Luczak

Gallaudet University Press
Washington, DC

Gallaudet University Press
Washington, DC 20002
http://gupress.gallaudet.edu

Library of Congress Cataloging-in-Publication Data
Luczak, Raymond, 1965–
Whispers of a savage sort, and other plays about the deaf American
experience / Raymond Luczak.
      p. cm.
ISBN 978-1-56368-420-3 (alk. paper)
I. Deaf–Drama.   I. Title.
   PS3562.U2554W47 2009
   812'.54–dc22   2009021816

♾The paper used in this publication meets the minimum requirements of
American National Standard for Information Sciences—Permanence of Paper
for Printed Library Materials, ANSI Z39.48-1984.

Contents

Foreword
Lurking from the Shadows   vii

Snooty   1

Love in My Veins   40

Doogle   81

Whispers of a Savage Sort   126

About the Author   177

Foreword
Lurking from the Shadows

WHEN IT COMES TO portraying Deaf people and their cultures onstage, very few hearing playwrights get it right. When Mark Medoff wrote his play *Children of a Lesser God*, he couched the love story within the then-raging political war between speech and sign. The input from his Deaf collaborator Phyllis Frelich on the long-standing historical struggle in Deaf education proved incalculable. His play still retains the dramatic power of its central conflict, but it does not feel as relevant today, particularly when many in the Deaf community have become increasingly inured to the reality that some Deaf adults have chosen to undergo cochlear implantation. The issue appears not to be so much about whether one can sign fluently in ASL, but whether one is willing to *accept* the increasingly divergent aftereffects of educational philosophies about how we interact with one another. I believe that is becoming the much larger story of what it means to be Deaf in America today. Whether the Deaf child today has a cochlear implant or wears a hearing aid—or even without either—is almost beside the point; I am more concerned with the issue of *community* in our future: Where are we Deaf adults going to be as a group when these Deaf children reach adulthood? Growing up, many of us did not always feel connected to our biological hearing families, so we have to wonder whether these Deaf children will feel the need to be part of something bigger and more meaningful as Deaf adults with the collective experience of hearing loss and communication struggles.

With the advent of hearing aid—and cochlear implantation—technologies, there is no doubt that when we examine the larger issue of what it means to be Deaf, we must examine how the forces of technology, particularly of those that are Internet- and mobile-based, are reshaping the Deaf community. My play *Doogle*, which combines the capital "D" as in the cultural label "Deaf" with the oft-used Google, follows a group of high school kids in a residential school for the Deaf. When I was commissioned by the Minnesota State Academy of the Deaf to write this play, the student performers requested that I incorporate the following elements: The dynamics of the TV show *The Brady Bunch*, reality shows, a hint of the film *The Breakfast Club*, and Internet-based teen technologies such as instant messages and email pagers, all at the same speed as the TV program *NYPD Blue* in a Deaf residential school setting. While working on the script, I suddenly realized that an interesting trend first mentioned twenty-five years ago in John Naisbitt's *Megatrends* had indeed come to pass: The more high-tech we become, the more high-touch we crave to be. The resulting play became a commentary on the changes in many Deaf people's behavior once they became Internet and pager junkies.

When I first wrote my comedy *Snooty* back in the late 1980s while I was a student at Gallaudet University, the big issue in Deaf education was the controversial use of Signing Exact English (SEE) in the classroom and its impact on American Sign Language (ASL). Michael Zuke, a hard of hearing seventh grader, has learned SEE to communicate, but he must now confront the fact that ASL has given Brutus, the ASL-fluent bully of his "hearing-impaired resources classroom," enough self-confidence and expressivity to enable him to incite the class behind their teacher's back. The constant switching between the reality of being called the clumsy SEE-using "snooty" by Michael's classmates and the fantasy of being the suave ASL-using Snooty Zook, the number one hit man on Chicago's South Side during the 1920s, was an homage to the days when I stood alone, mainstreamed all day long with the exception of three sessions a week with my speech therapist, by the brick walls of Ironwood Catholic Grade School. I knew that I was "hearing-impaired," but I did not have the tools necessary to articulate my inchoate instinct that there had to be more to life than being mocked because of my body aids which I wore in a bra-like harness underneath my shirt. Once I saw ASL and its culture at

Gallaudet in the summer of 1984, so much made intuitive sense that I've never looked back. It felt truly good to be Deaf, and it felt equally good not to stand out on a campus of so many Deaf students. Not being considered "special" was a truly liberating experience. It meant that not every single move I made was going to be noticed and made fun of, which gave me a little freedom to explore and experiment with fermenting new ideas on my own from a variety of books and classroom discussions on campus. The wallflower that I'd been nearly all my life was becoming far more assertive than I'd ever anticipated.

When I moved to New York City after graduating from Gallaudet in 1988, I rapidly became part of the adult Deaf community there, and I began to see stories not so readily apparent at first. For me as a gay man, AIDS became more and more of a health scare in the early 1990s, so such fears colored the way I observed the dynamics of people within their own relationships. That they were heterosexual or GLBT was of no concern to me, but how people interacted with each other imparted volumes that I'm still digesting to this very day. After the Houston-based theater company Illuminations Arts, then known as Illuminations Theater with the Deaf, invited me to write a play about AIDS as a response to World AIDS Day 2003, I found that creating the characters Hugh and Mindy to form the backbone of *Love in My Veins* was a genuine joy in spite of the play's heartbreaking tale. While I wanted to challenge the societal assumption that men were the usual culprits in spreading HIV infection to their wives, I explored how an oralist person might assimilate *into* the Deaf signing community through the prism of twenty-five years in a turbulent marriage between a Deaf oralist man and a culturally Deaf ASL-signing woman. I was equally interested in how trust, betrayal, and ultimately forgiveness could transform a Deaf couple's love for each other in a Deaf community who at times doesn't seem very supportive of them. Of all the love stories I've created so far for the stage, I would consider *Love in My Veins* my most passionate.

Whispers of a Savage Sort had been nothing more than an intriguing title that kicked around in the back of my head for years until one of my good friends expressed despair and frustration with how the local Deaf community had stabbed him in the back and turned against him through a simple yet willful misunderstanding. I decided to take out the "yet willful" part out of that situation and imagined how gossip and rumors could destroy the life of a good Deaf person who had grown up as an oralist and later married a Deaf-strong woman (not unlike Hugh and Mindy in *Love in My Veins,* which I would write five years later). But for *Whispers* I wanted to stretch my canvas to include a community of sorts and a variety of friendships even among only five characters. The production turned out to be a polarizing experience for both actors and audiences: Some of the performers were unaccustomed to the idea of possibly portraying a Deaf character who could be seen in a negative light, and some of the audience members were upset by my daring to portray the Deaf community in a disapproving light. Was I trying to be negative, as some claimed? No, I thought I was being honest.

Backstabbing is a major problem for many minorities struggling to advance themselves on the national level, which is another reason why I think it resonated with many people who saw the show. It was fascinating to see how evenly divided the audiences were every night during the question-and-answer sessions that followed each performance. I was thrilled because it meant that the audiences did not feel neutral about what happened onstage. No one could call the play simply "interesting." It meant that they had emotionally invested themselves in these characters so of course they felt *something.* Whether they liked the play or not was almost immaterial; whether they felt compelled to discuss their own reactions was much more important to me.

As a Deaf playwright, I feel even more obligated to ensure that my characters in a Deaf milieu are much more than cardboard cutouts or agitprops to support any particular political agenda. I did not want to preach. I felt it much more useful to instruct subversively through the guise of entertainment. I also wanted to aim for a more universality of my Deaf characters so that hearing audience members uninformed about deafness could still connect to the people onstage and see beyond their ears and hands. After a heated question-and-answer session following one of the performances of *Whispers of a Savage Sort*, a hearing black woman waved for an ASL interpreter to voice for her. She said that what she saw in the play onstage was no different from what went on in the hearing black company where she worked. I think such validation was one of my proudest moments as a playwright.

If *Whispers of a Savage Sort* could be said to present a moral about the Deaf community, I would say this: United we stand; divided we fall. With rare exceptions in the past two decades—the Deaf President Now movement in 1988 and the Unity for Gallaudet protest in 2006—the Deaf community hasn't coalesced politically on a national level. The divergent educational backgrounds that many of us Deaf people come from have ended up dividing us from each other, especially when it comes to communicating with one another. I would not be surprised if that turned out to be an unfortunate next chapter in the larger narrative of what it means to be a modern Deaf American. I offer these stories in this collection as a prelude to the near future.

Stories are littered everywhere, and it is up to us storytellers to rescue them and craft them in ways that make our audiences sit up and see the world in new ways. It is my hope that these stage plays will enable you to see that it is time for other Deaf playwrights to focus the spotlight on more of those untold stories lurking in the shadows.

Snooty

JEVON WHETTER DIRECTED THE world premiere production of *Snooty*, presented by the California School for the Deaf at Riverside at Deaf West Theater, Los Angeles, California, with the following cast on 8 May 1997.

MICHAEL/SNOOTY: Luis Torres
MS. GRAHAM/ALEXIS: Rebecca Goldenbaum
BRUNO/BRUTE: Javier Cruz
ELAINE/ELLIE: Evelina Gaina
MR. COPP/PRIEST: Art Caplan
PHIL/FIDO: Jonathan Martinez
ANDREW/ARROW: Michael Baker
TANGO CLUB GIRLS: Pauline Barrios, Erica Lanter, Arezo Moazezi
VOICE ACTORS: Canedy Knowles, Art Caplan

Dena was the production stage manager and Shawn Brimhall was the stage manager.

Adrian Blue directed a staged reading of *Snooty* at the Second Annual Worldwide and National Deaf Theater Conference, sponsored by the National Theater of the Deaf and presented at Wesleyan University's Theater 92, Middletown, Connecticut, on 16 July 1996.

MICHAEL/SNOOTY: Alex Jones
MS. GRAHAM/ALEXIS: Laura Murphy
BRUNO/BRUTE: John Kinstler
ELAINE/ELLIE: Rachel Judelson
MR. COPP/PRIEST: John Basinger
PHIL/FIDO: Lewis Merkin

ANDREW/ARROW: Willy Conley
OTHER: Robbi Allen Hunt

Patrick Graybill served as the script consultant and translator, and Kathy Holzwarth worked as the stage manager.

An earlier version of this play won first place in the New York Deaf Theater's 1990 Samuel Edwards Deaf Playwrights Competition.

STAGING CONSIDERATIONS

The Setting and the Players

MICHAEL's world: Smalltown USA, present
SNOOTY's world: Chicago's South Side, 1920s
(*Everyone is "deaf" so ASL is used as a matter of course*)

MICHAEL, a seventh-grader: hard of hearing; SEE/PSE with voice
SNOOTY, the best hit man for hire in Chicago

GRAHAM, his teacher: Hearing; SEE with voice
ALEXIS, a very mysterious woman

BRUNO, class bully: Deaf; ASL/PSE without voice
BRUTE, a second-rate hoodlum

ELAINE, classmate: Deaf; SEE with voice
ELLIE, Snooty's first girlfriend

COPP, principal: Hearing; voice only
PRIEST

PHIL, a classmate: Deaf; PSE without voice
FIDO, a fourth-rate hoodlum

ANDREW, classmate: Deaf; PSE without voice
ARROW, bartender/hoodlum

OTHERS* PSE/ASL/voice as needed
*OTHERS**
OTHERS are other actors with no lines in the scene but can be used as "background" or to give the crowd scenes some breadth. The more the merrier!

All players except GRAHAM and COPP should wear what seventh-graders would normally wear (T-shirts and jeans); but in Snooty's world, the more fedora hats and trench coats, the better. (Imaginary trench coats and fedora hats are fine too.) GRAHAM should wear a classy dark outfit with pumps. COPP should wear a navy blue business suit.

Michael and his classmates are seventh-graders who attend classes in a "hearing-impaired resources classroom" (Day school) at an otherwise hearing junior high school.

Classroom desks—or wooden crates—could be arranged for quick utilization to make each scene come alive: They can be turned into desks, chairs, beds, and so on. This can be easily accomplished with a larger cast onstage. Old 78s of Chicago jazz recordings could be played at a very low volume in the background throughout the play.

The phrase "Lights and set change" in stage directions means that the play has become Snooty's world—or Michael's—generally in a back-and-forth manner. Snooty's world could be lit in a film-noirish way with suggestions of lingering smoke; flashlights can be highly effective. Michael's world could be a little too harshly lit, perhaps by rods of fluorescent light above. Because the desks—or crates—can be moved around in so many ways, set changes can be accomplished at the same time as "lights and set change." But this is entirely up to the director. There is no intermission.

Because Snooty's world is rather like a cartoon, stylized stage business (e.g., the way cigarettes and pistols are held) should be used in the fantasy sequences.

The character "Snooty" has no name sign; his name is simply fingerspelled. Also, because most Deaf people find Signing Exact English (SEE) difficult to understand, some incorporation of ASL may prove helpful. Although I haven't seen the book in years, one may do well to consult Gerilee Gustason and Esther Zawolkow's *Signing Exact English*, a dictionary of SEE signs for "translation" suggestions.

[Lights open on where OTHERS are playing Cops and Robbers outside on the playground. MICHAEL skirts around the action, looking for a natural break into their game. Finally BRUNO shoots PHIL, and PHIL falls to the ground.

Lights change to a sleazy alleyway: OTHERS, including FIDO, are shooting at each other big-time, and finally the shootout stops when SNOOTY lifts his lapels and strides forward. With his eyes alert, SNOOTY is poised with his gun. Suddenly a gun goes off: SNOOTY catches the bullet in his fist as it whizzes past, and inspects it.]

SNOOTY: Cheap. Hah!

[SNOOTY is about to continue when he notices something in the distance. He then approaches the imaginary dead body.]

SNOOTY: Poppa? (*Glances around.*) Poppa . . . ?

[SNOOTY turns around with great suspicion just as lights change back to the playground. MICHAEL approaches BRUNO and OTHERS as PHIL gets up. BRUNO pushes MICHAEL aside.]

BRUNO: (*To PHIL.*) That was a good dead. C'mon, let's do it again.
PHIL: (*Rubs his buttocks.*) I'm sore all over.
MICHAEL: Unh, can I play a cop?
BRUNO: You? You're not tough like a cop.
MICHAEL: I can do it.
ANDREW: We can always shoot him down.
BRUNO: He's a sissy.
MICHAEL: No, I'm not.
ANDREW: Then why do you carry around books all the time?
BRUNO: He doesn't want to play dirty.
MICHAEL: I do—

[The morning bell rings. Ms. GRAHAM approaches them.]

GRAHAM: Come on. It's time for our first class. History.

[OTHERS mope their way into their classroom. MICHAEL lags behind and sits down.]

GRAHAM: Good morning, everyone.

ALL: Good morning, Ms. Graham.

GRAHAM: Thank you. Now, let's have each one of you tell us what you did last weekend. Phil?

PHIL: I watched TV. It was okay.

GRAHAM: Do you remember which show it was?

PHIL: No. But it was closed-captioned.

GRAHAM: That's wonderful. Andrew?

ANDREW: My dad and I went out to Big Boy's. They have real good malts.

GRAHAM: Not "real good." Really good. (*ANDREW nods; smiles.*) Elaine?

ELAINE: My sister took me to the zoo. We saw the new baby white bear.

GRAHAM: Did he look like that picture over there?

[OTHERS look up at the imaginary picture.]

ELAINE: He was a lot bigger than that. He looked happy with his mother.

GRAHAM: That's wonderful. Bruno?

BRUNO: My parents' friends came over and we all had a great barbecue in the backyard. (*Beat.*) Everyone was deaf so I understood everyone.

GRAHAM: We all know you come from a deaf family.

BRUNO: That's very important.

MICHAEL: You mean everyone talks the way you do?

BRUNO: Yeah. After two weeks here, you're still snooty.

GRAHAM: Bruno. Some people are not as lucky as you. Do you understand?

BRUNO: Yeah.

GRAHAM: Thank you. Michael?

MICHAEL: I watched a movie last night.

GRAHAM: What was it called?

MICHAEL: *The Man No One Knew*. It was pretty good.

PHIL: Was it closed-captioned?

MICHAEL: No. But I could follow the story.

BRUNO: Liar. He's just snooty.

GRAHAM: Bruno. (*To MICHAEL.*) He'll learn.

BRUNO: Never!

GRAHAM: We should begin our first class now. Please open your history books to page 74.

[*While OTHERS open the book and find the right page with GRAHAM checking to make sure everyone's on the same page, GRAHAM turns to MICHAEL.*]

GRAHAM: You can finish the next chapter in your book if you want.

[*BRUNO intercepts GRAHAM on her way back to her desk.*]

BRUNO: Why do you have to talk special to him? You treat him like he's a genius.

GRAHAM: Well, some people are better at sports than others; it's the same way with history. Michael happens to be very good with history.

BRUNO: But that doesn't mean you have to talk to him real special-like.

GRAHAM: (*Chooses to ignore BRUNO's remark.*) Could someone tell me why the 1920s was such an important time?

ANDREW: No one was allowed to drink beer.

GRAHAM: Very good, Andrew. (*To PHIL.*) Why did that happen, Phil?

PHIL: I dunno.

[*BRUNO kicks PHIL from behind and signs "Stupid!" (on the forehead).*]

GRAHAM: Andrew?

ANDREW: Some people thought drinking was bad.

GRAHAM: Elaine. What else happened at that time?

ELAINE: A lot of gangsters came to power. They ran a lot of speakeasies. They were like bars except they were hidden.

GRAHAM: Very good! And—

[Mr. COPP knocks on an imaginary door near them and hands GRA-HAM a note; he exits. She reads the note, and then turns to OTHERS.]

GRAHAM: Excuse me, I have to go out in the hallway for a minute. I don't want any horsing around, okay?

[OTHERS nod—but the second she and COPP go offstage, BRUNO runs to MICHAEL's desk and grabs his textbook.]

MICHAEL: Hey! Give it back.
BRUNO: You're too snooty for this class.

[MICHAEL leaps around BRUNO, trying to get back his textbook. Suddenly BRUNO tosses the book to ANDREW. MICHAEL runs to AN-DREW, who then tosses the book to PHIL. MICHAEL then chases PHIL around the classroom. ANDREW finds this hilarious. ANDREW laughs at the spectacle of poor little PHIL running up and down. Suddenly, ELAINE wrings the book out of PHIL's hands.]

PHIL: Hey! That's mine.
ANDREW: You're no fun.
ELAINE: *(Hands the book to MICHAEL.)* It belongs to him.
MICHAEL: Thank you.
BRUNO: *(To ELAINE.)* You got a problem or what?
ELAINE: We shouldn't fight all the time—
BRUNO: There goes our Goody Two-Shoes again.
ELAINE: I can be bad if I want to be.

[While ELAINE goes off to her desk, MICHAEL sits down at his desk.]

ANDREW: Oooh. That should be fun.
PHIL: Look at Michael.

[BRUNO struts over to MICHAEL's desk, and OTHERS except ELAINE converge around him.]

BRUNO: You a coward?
MICHAEL: No. I just think standing around and arguing is a waste of time.

BRUNO: If Elaine's our Goody Two-Shoes, then maybe you're our Goody Four-Eyes.

MICHAEL: I don't wear glasses.

BRUNO: All snooty people do.

MICHAEL: I'm not what you think I am.

[GRAHAM enters the classroom. OTHERS scatter back to their desks.]

GRAHAM: What happened here?

[Silence.]

GRAHAM: (To MICHAEL.) Would you feel better if we talked in private? (Beat.) Come on. (Gives OTHERS a look of warning.)

[While GRAHAM and MICHAEL talk in the hallway, OTHERS crowd together and press their faces against the door window, "eavesdropping" on GRAHAM and MICHAEL's conversation.]

GRAHAM: I'm sorry if they're giving you such a hard time.

MICHAEL: (Quietly.) Well . . .

GRAHAM: I'm really worried about you. You're in a new town, a new home, a new school, and . . . (Sighs.) I'm still sorry about your father. He shouldn't have gone off like that. He should feel honored to have you as his son.

MICHAEL: It's all right.

GRAHAM: Are you?

MICHAEL: (Beat.) I wish I could—(Notices BRUNO making faces at him.)

[MICHAEL looks off into the distance as lights and set change to the Tango Club, a notorious gangster hangout. OTHERS sit and hang about; BRUTE comes up to SNOOTY sitting by himself at a table.]

BRUTE: Hey. Can I talk some business wit' you?

SNOOTY: Hah! No. I'm waitin' for my dame.

BRUTE: I just want a vacation. A short one, please.

SNOOTY: I never take time off from bein' Snooty, so should you take time off from bein' Brute?

BRUTE: Hey, whatever you say.

[Just as BRUTE slinks away to his buddies nearby, ALEXIS walks pro-vocatively and gracefully into the bar. SNOOTY, nursing his drink, merely watches the ladies' restroom.]

BRUTE: Whoo! (*Nudges FIDO when ALEXIS passes by.*) Lookit her.
FIDO: (*Almost pants.*) Yeah! Yeah . . .

[OTHERS except ELLIE slowly converge around ALEXIS when she strides to where ARROW is bartending.]

ALEXIS: I'd like a Pink Lady.
ARROW: You would?
ALEXIS: I'm thirsty.
ARROW: Who said you're the only one thirsty around here? (*Grins as he gestures mixing ALEXIS's drink.*) There you go, ma'am.
ALEXIS: Thank you.

[ALEXIS turns her attention to the rest of the bar until she notices SNOOTY. ARROW catches the direction of ALEXIS's gaze.]

ARROW: (*Reverently.*) That's Snooty, the baddest guy on the Loop.
ALEXIS: Snooty?
ARROW: (*Blocks SNOOTY's view so he can't see what ARROW might say.*) He's the best in Chicago for any dirty job you want done . . . (*Glances back.*) If you got the dough.
ALEXIS: (*Glances at OTHERS standing around her.*) Then what's he doing here in a dump like this?

[OTHERS slink away.]

ARROW: Anything wrong with hangin' out?

[ELLIE returns from the bathroom. SNOOTY stands up to greet ELLIE. ALEXIS tries not to reveal interest in SNOOTY.]

ELLIE: Now I'm all powdered for the evening.

[SNOOTY holds ELLIE's chin and then notices past her ALEXIS drinking all by herself.]

SNOOTY: Who's that?

ELLIE: What? Don't even look at her!

SNOOTY: You ain't my mother.

ELLIE: But we're engaged!

SNOOTY: Relax. (*Keeps staring at ALEXIS.*)

ELLIE: Look at me. Aren't you going to follow your promise to—

SNOOTY: I don't wanna be told what to do, okay?

ELLIE: But if you're going to be my husband—

SNOOTY: Ellie, what am I gonna do at home if I quit? Sit in my rocking chair all day long? (*Scoffs.*) Hey, it's the Roarin' Twenties.

ELLIE: Don't you ever love me?

SNOOTY: (*Beat.*) Sometimes.

ELLIE: I know you better than you think.

SNOOTY: Come off it.

ELLIE: It's true. Deep down you're still a boy.

SNOOTY: I'm a man, got it?

[*SNOOTY moves ELLIE aside and approaches ALEXIS.*]

SNOOTY: You new in these parts?

ALEXIS: I'm visiting. You run this place?

SNOOTY: Could if I wanted to. (*Beat.*) Would you like a seat?

ALEXIS: Yes, please.

[*SNOOTY snaps his fingers, and both BRUTE and FIDO bring forth chairs for them. ELLIE blocks ALEXIS by sitting down in her chair.*]

SNOOTY: Make way for the lady!

ELLIE: I'm not moving. You're not keeping your promise.

ALEXIS: What's that?

ELLIE: We're getting married.

ALEXIS: Oooh. I should really leave.

[*ALEXIS is about to saunter off but SNOOTY grabs her elbow.*]

SNOOTY: Oh, no. Stay.

ELLIE: Why can't I stay?

SNOOTY: Because you say the same old things.

ELLIE: Sissy things?

SNOOTY: Get out!

ELLIE: You're not perfect. (*Gets up.*) You'll be sorry.

SNOOTY: Lemme inform you: I don't make promises that easily.

ELLIE: Then keep them.

SNOOTY: I'll keep them when we're married.

ELLIE: Oh, sure. Now I'll never trust you.

SNOOTY: Thought you knew I can't trust anyone, not in my business. (*To ALEXIS.*) Please.

[*ELLIE struts off in a huff. ALEXIS sits down.*]

ALEXIS: Well, thank you. Where've I seen you before?

SNOOTY: Who cares?

[*SNOOTY sits down. ARROW brings him another drink, and SNOOTY nods thanks.*]

ALEXIS: You're the face everyone knows, but hasn't seen in the papers yet.

SNOOTY: Yeah. You could say that.

ALEXIS: You don't show much, do you?

SNOOTY: The more cards I keep to my chest, the better.

ALEXIS: I see. You in the protection business?

SNOOTY: What are you runnin' away from?

ALEXIS: Nothing.

SNOOTY: Then why ask?

ALEXIS: You're fascinating.

SNOOTY: I prefer to stay hidden at night. (*Stands up and walks to where MICHAEL once stood; ALEXIS follows.*) That's my nature.

[*Lights change to the front of the classroom door. GRAHAM and MICHAEL are standing where OTHERS have returned to standing and "eavesdropping" on their conversation.*]

GRAHAM: You wish you could what?

MICHAEL: Nothing.

[COPP walks by in the hallway.]

GRAHAM: Excuse me. (*To COPP.*) What?
COPP: You have an emergency message. Here.

[GRAHAM reads it while COPP exits. GRAHAM reenters the classroom. OTHERS rush back to their desks.]

GRAHAM: I'm sorry, but I have to make a very important phone call. I'll be right back, so please read up until page 76.

[With GRAHAM gone, OTHERS gather around MICHAEL.]

BRUNO: Look at the size of his head. It's growing bigger every day, and then—
MICHAEL: My head isn't big.
ANDREW: Maybe if we rub it down, his head'll shrink. Maybe.
PHIL: Great idea!

[PHIL grabs MICHAEL's head and begins rubbing it.]

ELAINE: Why can't you stop?

[But no one heeds her.]

BRUNO: Hey. My turn now.
ANDREW: Look at his hair! His head is letting out some smelly air. Eeeuw.

[MICHAEL struggles, nearly kicks.]

PHIL: You ticklish?

[MICHAEL pushes ANDREW and BRUNO—just barely—away from himself. OTHERS stare at him.]

ANDREW: What's the matter?
MICHAEL: I want to be friends with you—
PHIL: You read too many books.
BRUNO: Too many books mean a big ego. That's what my dad says.
MICHAEL: That's not true.

PHIL: How do you know?

MICHAEL: I just know, okay?

BRUNO: See? He's snooty.

[BRUNO shoves MICHAEL, but he almost falls. He recovers just in time as lights change back to later that night at the Tango Club. BRUTE "catches" SNOOTY, but SNOOTY pushes him aside and grabs ALEXIS instead for another round of tangoing. When either of them talks, the tango stops completely, but in between they pick up their tango as if nothing's happened.]

SNOOTY: Never thought we'd get close this fast. (Beat.) The stars are bright and shinin' on us tonight. Suddenly everything's clear to me now, and there you are, with me. (Spins her around and squeezes her.)

ALEXIS: You're holding me . . . a little bit too tight.

[ALEXIS spins away from SNOOTY.]

SNOOTY: Maybe your dress is a bit tight. (Rasps.) Loosen it if you want.

ALEXIS: Snooty!

SNOOTY: Always one step ahead. That's my motto.

ALEXIS: You don't know me yet.

SNOOTY: I'm waitin'.

ALEXIS: Looks like the world's all yours.

SNOOTY: Not until you become mine.

[The tango stops.]

ALEXIS: Oh?

SNOOTY: I'm a man of honor. Anyone'll tell you that.

ALEXIS: You're a gentleman?

SNOOTY: Yeah. And you're a lady. (Beat.) What's your name?

ALEXIS: You promised not to ask.

SNOOTY: You know mine: Snooty Zook.

ALEXIS: You promised!

SNOOTY: Well?

ALEXIS: Fine. (*Beat.*) I'm Alexis. Nick Orlansky's daughter.

SNOOTY: You—? (*Beat.*) You're a jinx minx.

ALEXIS: Wait a minute. Where are you going?

SNOOTY: You know.

[ALEXIS runs after SNOOTY, and he looks down at her hand touching him. She finally lets go.]

ALEXIS: I'm really sorry.

SNOOTY: Are you? (*Beat.*) Did you kill my Poppa?

ALEXIS: Everyone knows he had too many shady business deals.

SNOOTY: Did you?

ALEXIS: What?

SNOOTY: Did you kill my Poppa?

ALEXIS: Would I be so stupid to come here if I did? Of course not.

SNOOTY: I suppose you're right.

ALEXIS: You don't believe me?

[ALEXIS pulls out her gun and flings it at SNOOTY, who nearly bends over from the gun's weight hitting his stomach just as lights change back to the classroom. GRAHAM reenters just as the morning recess bell rings. She checks her watch and sighs; she doesn't really notice OTHERS watching MICHAEL recover himself.]

GRAHAM: Recess time.

[OTHERS go out of the classroom to the playground. ELAINE goes off by herself and reads an imaginary book a distance away from OTHERS trying to decide what to play. PHIL notices a loose shoelace, and bends down to tie it. MICHAEL walks over to PHIL.]

MICHAEL: How did you get to be Bruno's friend?

PHIL: Move away.

MICHAEL: I'm not a bad person.

PHIL: Yes, you are.

MICHAEL: I read books. So what?

[PHIL finishes retying and stands up.]

PHIL: It means you're snooty. You always have to show everyone how much you know.

[PHIL runs off to BRUNO and ANDREW.]

ANDREW: What were you doing with Mikey?
PHIL: He wants to be our friend.
BRUNO: He does? (*To MICHAEL.*) Get over here.
MICHAEL: What?
BRUNO: You want to be our friend?
MICHAEL: Sure.
BRUNO: Then you have to squeeze Elaine's boobs.
MICHAEL: Do I have to?
ANDREW: Yeah. Our friends got to show who's got real guts.
MICHAEL: (*Beat.*) Okay.
BRUNO: You can't fake it now. We have to see how you do it.

[MICHAEL nods and walks slowly. ELAINE looks up from reading her book.]

ELAINE: What's wrong?
MICHAEL: Unh.
ELAINE: (*Stands up.*) You okay?
MICHAEL: Um. Could you close your eyes?
ELAINE: Why?
MICHAEL: Please.
ELAINE: You're not going to hurt me?
MICHAEL: Of course not.
ELAINE: If you say so.

[ELAINE closes her eyes. MICHAEL quickly jabs her just above her breasts.]

ELAINE: Ow!

[BRUNO, ANDREW, and PHIL guffaw at ELAINE. She catches this.]

ELAINE: Who told you to do that?
MICHAEL: I-I did.
ELAINE: I thought you were my friend.

[*The recess bell suddenly rings. COPP walks by and notices OTHERS still playing.*]

COPP: (*Voices and gestures.*) Hey! You all go into class now.

[*OTHERS start racing back into the classroom.*]

BRUNO: (*To MICHAEL.*) Good, but you didn't squeeze enough.

[*MICHAEL tags behind OTHERS. BRUNO checks the hallway for GRAHAM, but she's nowhere in sight. He stands behind GRAHAM's desk.*]

BRUNO: Hey, hey, hey. I got a cool story to tell you. I saw a great movie last night.

ANDREW: Oh, good. He tells his stories real good.

BRUNO: Shh, shh. (*If the following story can be conveyed without relying on voicing, all the better.*) "A sleek black limo came riding up the street in a small town. No one could see inside, and everyone moved away from the car: No one knew who was inside that car. All of a sudden one of the windows rolled down slowly. Silence. No one dared move. What was inside that car? Finally, a boy came right up to the window and tried to lift himself by putting his fingers right on top of the rolled window. The window looked like it was going to break, but no. The boy got himself up and finally squinted inside. He couldn't see anything. Finally his eyes got used to the darkness inside the car, and suddenly—there was a long shotgun touching the boy's forehead. Then suddenly—his brains splattered all over the sidewalk. The window rolled up and simply went out of sight." That was how the movie began. My jaw just dropped.

ELAINE: Oh, that's so stupid. (*To MICHAEL.*) What did you think?

MICHAEL: I couldn't understand all of it.

BRUNO: That's because you're so snooty.

MICHAEL: No, I'm not. I'm still learning signs—

BRUNO: Snooty, snooty, snooty.

MICHAEL: But you're a good storyteller.

BRUNO: You don't even know my language.

MICHAEL: I can learn by watching.

BRUNO: Snooty people can't learn my language. It's not brain candy.

[GRAHAM strolls in to catch BRUNO fleeing from her front desk.]

GRAHAM: You come right here.

BRUNO: (*Uses the "nose" sign; not voiced.*) Shit.

GRAHAM: I don't understand what you've just said.

BRUNO: You can't understand me? I can't understand you either. I can't follow your signing. Even my parents make fun of it. Like this. (*Demonstrates an example of exaggerated SEE.*) "Gravy." G-r-a-v-y. See?

GRAHAM: I'm sorry, but that's our method.

BRUNO: (*Signs with two "V" fingers hitting each other.*) Stupid.

GRAHAM: What did you mean by that?

BRUNO: (*Slowly so GRAHAM can read him.*) S-t-u-p-i-d.

GRAHAM: Are you calling me (*Mistakenly uses the sign for "intercourse."*) stupid?

[OTHERS laugh hysterically.]

BRUNO: No. Your way of signing is. (*To OTHERS, not voiced.*) Stupid-intercourse-stupid.

[Everyone except GRAHAM laughs even harder.]

GRAHAM: All right. Let's get back to work.

[While GRAHAM tries to find her place in her textbook, BRUNO makes a face at MICHAEL, and points to ELAINE; he pretends to be MICHAEL kissing ELAINE. She catches this.]

ELAINE: Hey!

GRAHAM: What's going on?

ELAINE: (*Stands up.*) Michael tried to grab my breasts.

GRAHAM: What—? When? (*Beat.*) Michael. Is it true? (*MICHAEL looks away.*) I'm really disappointed in you.

MICHAEL: (*Looks down, and then to ELAINE.*) I'm sorry.

[Lights and set change to ELLIE's house. SNOOTY stands suddenly before ELLIE.]

SNOOTY: I realize I been a real low-life. I didn't honor my loyalty to you.

ELLIE: So Alexis turned you away?

SNOOTY: Oh, no. I turned her away.

ELLIE: I'll never turn you away—

SNOOTY: No one does.

[SNOOTY walks back and forth.]

ELLIE: What happened?

SNOOTY: Why didn't anyone tell me about her?

ELLIE: Bet she wasn't here just for a "visit."

SNOOTY: Why was I so stupid?

ELLIE: It's all right.

SNOOTY: No, it's not. I have to know everything.

ELLIE: But you can't rule the whole world.

SNOOTY: Let's get married now.

ELLIE: Now? Why the hurry?

SNOOTY: We've been engaged long enough.

ELLIE: Six months?

SNOOTY: Why wait for a fancy church wedding?

ELLIE: I'm the kind of gal who marries only once in her life.

SNOOTY: I can bribe Father Joe into giving us the church on Saturday.

ELLIE: This Saturday?

SNOOTY: Sure. Why not? (*Grins.*)

ELLIE: With all the trimmings?

SNOOTY: I can afford anything you want.

[SNOOTY and ELLIE embrace.]

ELLIE: Now, who do we invite to the wedding?

SNOOTY: Everybody except her. (*Beat.*) Come on. I'll treat you to a fancy lunch.

[Lights and set change to the school cafeteria. MICHAEL and ELAINE give each other dirty looks; they are now carrying their lunch trays. OTHERS sit at a long table, eating lunch. MICHAEL sits at one end, and ELAINE doesn't even look at him as she sits down at the other end. BRUNO waves for ELAINE's attention.]

BRUNO: I thought Mikey was rude.

ELAINE: You don't know anything about respect.

ANDREW: Of course, we do. We like to say nice things.

PHIL: Yeah! Nice things for nice people.

ELAINE: Leave me alone.

BRUNO: You're sitting right there.

ELAINE: You can stare at your beautiful friends.

ANDREW: Hey. We're not sissies.

[ELAINE ignores their imitations of limp wrists and subsequent guffaws. MICHAEL looks away when ELAINE gives him a hard look. BRUNO flings a pea at MICHAEL's face.]

BRUNO: Maybe Mikey's gonna be a girl!

ANDREW: Where's your lipstick?

MICHAEL: I don't have any.

PHIL: Maybe you can take some from Ms. Graham's purse.

MICHAEL: Very funny.

[ANDREW suddenly slaps his palm on MICHAEL's lips, and then pretends it's a "hot potato" and passes it on to BRUNO, who then passes it on to PHIL. PHIL slaps MICHAEL's "kiss" on ELAINE's lips. Offended, ELAINE leaves the cafeteria.]

ANDREW: Who's your girlfriend?

MICHAEL: I don't have a girlfriend.

BRUNO: Oh yes, you do. The girl with the big boobs.

MICHAEL: She's not big.

PHIL: You just touched her.

BRUNO: *(Gets up.)* We'll give you one more chance to be our friend.

ANDREW: This better be good.

MICHAEL: What if I don't want to?

BRUNO: Then you're a sissy.

PHIL: Snooty sissy! Snooty sissy!

[BRUNO, PHIL, and ANDREW guffaw. MICHAEL gets up to leave.]

BRUNO: Don't leave if you want to be in all the fun.

MICHAEL: What do you want me to do?

ANDREW: Ooh, lots of things.

MICHAEL: One more time, and then that's it.

ANDREW: We test each other every day. You know that.

PHIL: Yeah! And it's lots and lots of fun!

MICHAEL: Okay. What do you want me to do?

BRUNO: Let's see. (Glances around for an idea.) Oh. You can flip four butter squares to the ceiling. One for each of us. And don't get caught.

MICHAEL: Oh, that explains those spots up there—

ANDREW: How do you think Phil got to be one of us?

MICHAEL: Four? (Glances around and then reaches for a spoon.) Should be easy.

[MICHAEL puts a butter square on his spoon, and glances around. The coast is clear: MICHAEL flicks the spoon. BRUNO, PHIL, and ANDREW guffaw at the sight of butter sticking to the ceiling. MICHAEL glows.]

PHIL: Three left!

[MICHAEL puts another butter square on his spoon and flicks it quickly. Even MICHAEL joins in their contagiously raucous laughter. Another flick of spoon and butter, and they pound their table with helpless laughter.]

BRUNO: Look at that. Three of them sticking out like droopy boobs—

GRAHAM: Like what?

[MICHAEL looks up to see GRAHAM standing right next to him.]

GRAHAM: Michael, you've broken a rule here.

MICHAEL: I'm sorry.

GRAHAM: I believe Bruno's setting a bad example.

BRUNO: I'm not a bad person.

GRAHAM: We're all going to his office right now and hear your stories.

[MICHAEL goes first, followed by OTHERS; GRAHAM is last. Lights and set change to the Tango Club. OTHERS follow SNOOTY to his table.]

SNOOTY: Should I tell you a story?

ARROW: Hey. Your next drink's free if you tell it.

SNOOTY: All right. (Assumes a melodramatic pose.) "One night I was drivin' along the street when I saw this beautiful dame struttin' by herself. Her clothes were awfully tight for a classy dame. I thought I knew all the girls of her kind thereabouts. When I stopped, she turned and looked at me with laser-beam eyes. She smiled, and I gave her a nasty grin. She came up to my car window and blew a kiss at me. I kept laughin' and laughin' at her. Then she pulled out a gun from inside her dress and aimed it at my chest. I laughed and laughed. Then she started laughin' too until she pulled the trigger. The bullet bounced right off my chest. She obviously didn't know who I was, and she didn't know I always wore my bulletproof vest."

FIDO: Wow.

BRUTE: Don't be such a dog.

[ALEXIS strolls in. SNOOTY looks up. ELLIE stands up, and SNOOTY pushes her aside.]

ELLIE: Wait. Don't you have any feelings for other people?

SNOOTY: I shoot people for money. I treat dames like dirt. Got that? (Scoffs.) I'm surprised that people look up to me.

ELLIE: You're like a god. Everything has to be putty in your hands.

SNOOTY: I ain't no sissy. (Beat.) Any more stories?

ELLIE: I'm leaving.

SNOOTY: But you'll be back for more. You just don't have my nerve.

ELLIE: That's what you like to think. (*Beat.*) Is the wedding still on?

SNOOTY: (*Beat.*) Yeah.

ELLIE: Oh, right.

[ELLIE moves to the side, eyeing ALEXIS the entire time.]

BRUTE: Tell us about Nick Orlansky. (*ALEXIS stiffens at the mention of her father's name.*) The one who died horribly two weeks ago.

SNOOTY: (*To ALEXIS.*) It's about your Poppa. You'll have to forgive me on this one.

ALEXIS: Maybe that's why your father was killed. (*Beat.*) An eye for an eye.

ELLIE: You don't have to watch. You can leave.

ALEXIS: (*Stands up.*) Everything's evened out. No more bad blood, right?

[ALEXIS exits.]

SNOOTY: Hm. Okay, that's that.

ARROW: (*Mixes a drink.*) You got another free drink coming right at ya.

SNOOTY: Someone's shot Poppa and you know what that means? I'm goin' after whoever did it. He's gonna pay!

[Lights and set change to COPP's office. COPP stands before MICHAEL, BRUNO, PHIL, and ANDREW; he gestures as appropriate to punctuate his "lecture."]

COPP: Boys, you do understand that flipping butter pats on the ceiling is against the rules. Now, you're all going to stay in my office until the end of lunch break, and you are to stay quiet.

BRUNO: (*More gestures than signs.*) But we didn't do anything! Michael did.

COPP: You didn't stop him.

MICHAEL: They asked me to—

COPP: I'm not interested in fingerpointing. You're all guilty. Now you all stay quiet.

[COPP exits. BRUNO taps on MICHAEL's shoulder.]

BRUNO: It's all your fault.

MICHAEL: You asked me to.

BRUNO: You weren't supposed to get caught.

PHIL: (Interrupts.) He did three. That's not too bad—

ANDREW: Why do you have to be nice all the time?

MICHAEL: (To BRUNO.) I'm sorry, okay?

PHIL: (To ANDREW.) He's not trying to hurt anyone.

BRUNO: What's going on?

ANDREW: I think we have a new sissy here. (Indicates PHIL.)

BRUNO: Come on. Phil makes a great pal. That's why he's one of us.

MICHAEL: You mean Phil didn't do the butter squares before?

[PHIL looks guilty.]

ANDREW: Too late now. We're here.

BRUNO: Maybe we can escape.

PHIL: Then we'll get real grounded.

MICHAEL: I'm not listening to you ever again.

BRUNO: We'll make you watch us, all right.

ANDREW: Let's give him one more chance, huh?

[ANDREW looks out COPP's office.]

PHIL: Like what?

ANDREW: What if Mikey could steal some panties from the girls' locker room?

MICHAEL: By the gym? Oh no, no.

ANDREW: (To BRUNO.) Remember?

BRUNO: Oooh, that's so cool.

MICHAEL: I'm not doing that.

BRUNO: Oh, come on. Don't be a sissy.

MICHAEL: No. No. No.

BRUNO: This is not a game, you know.

[Lights and set change into a casino. SNOOTY stands with OTHERS around a table, and he tosses the dice.]

SNOOTY: Whoo! Yeah!

[ALEXIS wanders in, and finds SNOOTY.]

SNOOTY: I thought we broke up. What're you doin' here?
ALEXIS: Don't I have a right to be here?
SNOOTY: Dames ain't allowed here.
ALEXIS: Then what are these girls doing here?
SNOOTY: (*Shrugs.*) That's what they are—just girls.
ALEXIS: I've been hearing rumors about you. (*Beat.*) You'll get killed!
SNOOTY: Who?
ALEXIS: I don't know. I just fear for your life.
SNOOTY: Nah, don't worry. I still got my bulletproof vest.
ALEXIS: Sometimes you're too prepared.
SNOOTY: Go home, Alexis. I can take care of myself.
ALEXIS: But—
SNOOTY: This place ain't safe.
ALEXIS: You don't understand. I want to be with you, Snooty.
SNOOTY: I am a dangerous man . . . and this is a dangerous place.

[Lights and set change. MICHAEL looks both ways before he steps out of COPP's office; the coast is clear. He rushes to the opposite end of the stage, and holds himself flat against the corner.

The BOYS snicker, but stop when they see GRAHAM coming. Then they return to their seats and feign nonchalance. GRAHAM strolls past with her lunch bag, not even noticing that MICHAEL is standing right by her and holding his breath. Finally she exits.]

[MICHAEL looks both ways before he cautiously opens the door to the girls' locker room. Nothing. Nobody. He steps in quickly and glances around. He scurries up and down the lockers, and finally finds a pair of abandoned panties.

MICHAEL tries to stuff them into his pockets, but his pockets are too small. MICHAEL glances around himself, and then catches himself in a mirror: Eureka!

MICHAEL stuffs the panties into his armpits under his shirt. His arms are now clasped to his sides, but it's better than his tiny pockets.

MICHAEL cautiously opens the door and checks the hallway. Nobody. MICHAEL runs out, and is about to turn the corner when he notices GRAHAM coming back from her lunch. MICHAEL flattens himself against the corner. The BOYS watch this.

This time GRAHAM catches MICHAEL. The BOYS, of course, try not to guffaw.]

GRAHAM: What are you doing here?

MICHAEL: Unh? I'm . . . I had to go bathroom.

GRAHAM: I had to go to . . . *the* bathroom. You mustn't let your
    English get sloppy. (*Beat.*) You haven't answered my question.

MICHAEL: I really had to go.

GRAHAM: The boys' bathroom is down the hall. That way.

[MICHAEL tries not to fidget from the panties tucked in his armpits.]

GRAHAM: Are your arms all right?

MICHAEL: Er . . . Why?

GRAHAM: Your arms look a little tight.

MICHAEL: Oh. I'm sorry. I-I got confused.

GRAHAM: I'll check with Mr. Copp a little later on.

[GRAHAM exits. MICHAEL nods, and slips right into COPP's office.]

ANDREW: I can't believe it. Ms. Graham—

MICHAEL: I got two of them.

BRUNO: Let me see.

[MICHAEL pulls out the panties from under his shirt.]

ANDREW: Eeeuw. Just like his head.

PHIL: Hey. He did good.

[COPP happens to pop in and notices the panties. The BOYS scramble to their chairs.]

COPP: Hey. What's going on here?

[*It's clear from their expressions that BRUNO, PHIL, and ANDREW find him rather difficult to lipread; COPP gestures, as needed, along with his voice to make himself a little clearer.*]

MICHAEL: Unh, Bruno needed something to blow his nose on.

COPP: There are tissues over there. (*Grabs the panties from MICHAEL's hands; to BRUNO.*) Or would you rather blow your nose on these?

BRUNO: Unh. (*To MICHAEL.*) What's he exactly saying?

COPP: (*To MICHAEL.*) Where did you get these?

MICHAEL: I-I found them over there.

COPP: All right. (*Narrows his eyes on BRUNO.*) You're too good to your friends. But you still have to be quiet. (*Beat.*) Lunch break isn't over yet.

[*COPP looks distastefully at the panties, pulls out a bag from his desk, and drops the panties into the bag before exiting.*]

PHIL: (*To BRUNO; indicates MICHAEL.*) He defended you.

BRUNO: (*Stands up.*) He made me look like a jerk.

MICHAEL: I wasn't trying to—

PHIL: He proved himself.

BRUNO: You can't decide for me. I run this group.

MICHAEL: (*With braggadocio.*) Really?

BRUNO: Aaarrgh!

[*BRUNO lunges at MICHAEL and punches his nose out. MICHAEL crumples. PHIL looks up at BRUNO, who grabs some Kleenex from COPP's desk to wipe the blood off his fingers. MICHAEL is woozy from the punch.*]

PHIL: I thought he was one of us.

BRUNO: The way he talks. Ugh.

ANDREW: You're gonna be in deep trouble.

BRUNO: I don't care. I never liked this place anyway.

[COPP *rushes in and notices MICHAEL on the floor. He rushes back out in the hallway.*]

COPP: Nurse! Nurse! (*Beat; to GRAHAM.*) Oh, you. Come over here!

[*GRAHAM comes running in.*]

GRAHAM: Michael, are you okay? (*To BRUNO.*) Did you hit him? (*To OTHERS.*) Did he?

[*No one answers.*]

COPP: What's going on here?
GRAHAM: What do you think?

[*MICHAEL looks at his bloodied hand; he gets up. Lights and set change to the Tango Club. SNOOTY is still covering his nose when ELLIE comes scurrying over.*]

ELLIE: Oh! What happened to you?
SNOOTY: This sometimes happens when I have to negotiate. (*Beat.*) Thought this place would be perfect for business. (*Moans.*) Great atmosphere, you know?
ELLIE: Let me get something for your nose.
SNOOTY: No, I'll be fine. (*Moves to exit.*)
ELLIE: Wait a minute. Where are you going? Where's Brute?
SNOOTY: He went out for some fresh air.
ELLIE: He's supposed to be protecting you.
SNOOTY: Ahh. Another day, another shootout. Big deal.
ELLIE: But you've got to rest.

[*But it's too late. As SNOOTY strolls toward the other end of the stage, a gunshot goes off. SNOOTY gets shot in the arm. ELLIE runs out and helps SNOOTY to his chair back in the Tango Club.*]

ELLIE: You all right?
SNOOTY: Yeah. (*Beat.*) You see who shot me?
ELLIE: No. (*Glances around.*) Maybe Alexis's hiding nearby.

SNOOTY: Her? Nah. We're both evened out on both sides of our families.

ELLIE: I just hate your job.

SNOOTY: Nobody shoots Snooty down! Don'tcha worry 'bout that. (*Gets up.*)

ELLIE: You must see a doctor.

SNOOTY: No. I'll be fine. Really.

ELLIE: I don't care. (*Beat.*) I'll be back soon.

SNOOTY: Fine. Whatever. I'll come lookin' for you if I disappear.

ELLIE: Promise?

SNOOTY: With my heart. I'm Snooty.

[ELLIE goes off. BRUTE enters the Tango Club.]

SNOOTY: Brute! Where've you been?

BRUTE: Gee, that customer was a tough cookie. (*Notices SNOOTY's bleeding nose and arm.*) Hey. You all right?

SNOOTY: Yeah.

BRUTE: Who shot you? I'll get 'im for you if you want.

SNOOTY: When this heals, we'll talk. (*Beat.*) What you're here for?

BRUTE: I just wanna tell you something . . .

SNOOTY: What's up, buddy?

BRUTE: I can't lie to me no more.

SNOOTY: Don't tell me. I don't wanna know.

BRUTE: No. I've fallen for Alexis.

SNOOTY: Don't you think everybody has?

BRUTE: Snooty, it's not that. I think she's fallen for me too.

SNOOTY: (*Grabs BRUTE's lapels.*) Well, control yourself. Get outta town and never see her again.

BRUTE: Unh, I'm sorry. I'll never talk to her again. Look. I promise ya, I'll help ya when ya need some muscle, okay?

SNOOTY: Swell.

[SNOOTY exits the Tango Club, and sits down on a park bench. He feels his arm and winces. Lights and set change to the infirmary. MICHAEL is

sitting by himself when COPP enters. COPP speaks and gestures as needed.]

COPP: You all right?

MICHAEL: Yes.

COPP: Do you think you'll be all right back in class?

MICHAEL: Yes.

COPP: Are you sure? You have a lot of pride.

MICHAEL: A lot of what?

COPP: (*More slowly.*) Pride.

MICHAEL: What's that word?

COPP: Unh, it's the same as "proud."

MICHAEL: Proud. Yes.

COPP: I know you took those panties.

MICHAEL: What?

COPP: Panties. You've got to show women more respect than that.

[MICHAEL, not quite understanding COPP, nods.]

COPP: You have to be careful how you pick your friends. It's not about pride. It's about good feelings.

MICHAEL: (*Still not quite understanding him.*) Yes.

COPP: Good. Now come with me.

[MICHAEL follows COPP out of the infirmary. Lights and set change to the Tango Club. SNOOTY swaggers across the stage, and then addresses OTHERS.]

FIDO: You're alive? Everybody said you died in a hospital somewhere.

SNOOTY: I left early. (*Beat.*) Where's Brute?

[No one answers.]

SNOOTY: I thought you were my pals.

ARROW: We are.

FIDO: It's just that . . . Brute's been acting funny lately.

ARROW: Yeah. He doesn't even wanna drink scotch anymore.

SNOOTY: He orders Pink Ladies now?

ARROW: How did you know?

SNOOTY: I coulda been a great detective if I wanna be one. (*Beat.*) Oh, come on. You know me better than that. I ain't no scaredy-cat, and there you are, huddlin' together like a litter of kitties. I always protect my pals. Or my name would be worth nothin'.

[OTHERS trail behind him until lights and set change to the empty classroom. MICHAEL enters alone. GRAHAM looks up from correcting homework.]

GRAHAM: Are you all right?

MICHAEL: Yes.

GRAHAM: Well, it's recess time. You have fifteen minutes.

[MICHAEL nods and then goes offstage as OTHERS go through the motions of playing kickball. BRUNO kicks a home run and touches all bases. ELAINE gives an occasional "Oh-sure" look at their actions.]

BRUNO: I got it!

PHIL: He always gets home runs.

ANDREW: (*Laughs, to BRUNO.*) Hey, you were lucky.

[PHIL is about to kick the next ball. MICHAEL steps right in front to talk to BRUNO. ELAINE moves a little more closely to MICHAEL.]

BRUNO: What do you want?

MICHAEL: Can I have a turn?

ANDREW: (*Steps between PHIL and BRUNO.*) You're crazy. He just punched you out.

MICHAEL: I'm okay.

PHIL: He should be one of us.

BRUNO: Shut up!

MICHAEL: Let me play.

ANDREW: You know how to play?

MICHAEL: No, but I can always learn—

BRUNO: You're out.

MICHAEL: It's only a game.

BRUNO: Not if you play the way I do. I play it like life and death.

PHIL: That's why he's Bruno. (*Beat.*) He can have my turn.

MICHAEL: Really?

ANDREW: You can't give him your turn. He's not on our team.

PHIL: You stand over here—

BRUNO: You can't tell him what to do. I tell him what to do. Maybe I'll throw you out.

PHIL: You promised I'd be in forever!

MICHAEL: You break promises, too?

BRUNO: No.

PHIL: Then I'm in.

ANDREW: What about him?

MICHAEL: I can play.

[MICHAEL kicks the ball lamely.]

MICHAEL: Ah, shoot!

BRUNO: You didn't kick it far.

MICHAEL: (*To PHIL.*) Was Bruno's first kick a perfect one?

BRUNO: Shut up.

[ELAINE taps on BRUNO's shoulder.]

ELAINE: No. My brother taught Bruno how to play.

BRUNO: I don't like your brother anyway.

MICHAEL: (*Smugly.*) So you're not perfect either.

BRUNO: Get outta my way!

MICHAEL: No.

BRUNO: I'll punch you out again.

MICHAEL: Go ahead.

BRUNO: Oh, yeah? You "real-ly" mean that?

[Lights change. SNOOTY stands by himself, inhaling an imaginary cigarette and looking off into the distance. Suddenly BRUTE throws a punch at SNOOTY, but SNOOTY catches the punch like a baseball and twists BRUTE's arm so BRUTE is forced down to his knees. SNOOTY finishes his cigarette and finally looks down at BRUTE.]

SNOOTY: Some things are worth doin'. But this ain't one of 'em.

[Lights return to the playground. MICHAEL and BRUNO are standing and facing each other as before. MICHAEL backs off.]

MICHAEL: I changed my mind.
BRUNO: Sissy.
MICHAEL: No, I'm not.

[BRUNO jumps on MICHAEL, and they both fall.]

ANDREW: Ms. Graham's coming!
BRUNO: You won't squeal?

[MICHAEL shakes his head no.]

PHIL: You okay?
BRUNO: But we haven't finished this yet.
ANDREW: We can have a fight after school.
BRUNO: (*To MICHAEL.*) Agreed? Good. I'll come looking for you.

[BRUNO and OTHERS except ELAINE and MICHAEL go off to the opposite side of the stage.]

MICHAEL: Thank you.
ELAINE: What are friends for?
MICHAEL: I thought you didn't like me.
ELAINE: You'll learn.

[Embarrassed, MICHAEL says nothing. By now GRAHAM's come to them, and notices BRUNO and OTHERS.]

GRAHAM: (*To ALL.*) Time to go in.

[ELAINE and OTHERS go first into the classroom, and MICHAEL is about to join them when BRUNO shoves MICHAEL to the side.]

BRUNO: I got friends. Real friends, you know?

[BRUNO goes off. Lights and set change to the Tango Club. SNOOTY, ELLIE, FIDO, and ARROW toast with their shots of liquor before gulping. Meanwhile, BRUTE strolls in with his sore fist.]

BRUTE: Who do you think you are?

SNOOTY: Who else?

ELLIE: Can't you see he's busy?

BRUTE: (*To SNOOTY.*) You wanna duel?

SNOOTY: (*Takes out his own imaginary gun.*) Fine. Let's move it real quick. I don't wanna miss my dinner.

[*BRUTE and SNOOTY stand face-to-face as OTHERS move away into the background. BRUTE and SNOOTY pace backwards from each other to both ends of the stage; their eyes do not waver from each other's. BRUTE and SNOOTY check their guns one last time.*]

ELLIE: Snooty! Don't.

BRUTE: See that? She thinks you can't win—

SNOOTY: (*Clenches his teeth.*) Don't be too sure.

ELLIE: Can't you just stop and be friends?

BRUTE: How can we? Only one of us can have you.

[*ALEXIS strolls onstage and then notices: Snooty and Brute against each other?*]

ALEXIS: Hey. What's going on?

ELLIE: Why are you here now?

ALEXIS: I like checking up on my friends. (*To SNOOTY.*) Stop this, the two of you!

SNOOTY: That's what I'm doin'.

BRUTE: Yeah. Me too.

[*SNOOTY and BRUTE aim their imaginary guns swiftly at each other, and the two guns go off with a flash. OTHERS cover their eyes as BRUTE collapses. SNOOTY stands as in a receding fog.*]

ALEXIS: Oh!—

[*ALEXIS runs to BRUTE, and OTHERS gather behind them.*]

ELLIE: Snooty! You won again.

SNOOTY: (*To BRUTE now writhing in pain.*) You forgot to check for my bulletproof vest. (*To ALEXIS.*) Let's go.

ALEXIS: You can't leave him here like this.

SNOOTY: So? I won. You have to come with me.

ELLIE: Wait. What about me?

SNOOTY: Have you ever thought I might settle a deal with her?

ALEXIS: But—but . . .

SNOOTY: What? What? Tell me the truth. (*Beat.*) You two been plottin' somethin' against me?

ALEXIS: You're imagining things.

SNOOTY: He coulda shot Poppa. Whaddya think?

ELLIE: Let's go.

SNOOTY: No. This is private.

[SNOOTY pulls ALEXIS along and they stand outside the Tango Club. ALEXIS pulls out her pack of cigarettes.]

ALEXIS: Cigarette?

SNOOTY: Thanks.

[As SNOOTY takes a cigarette, they look into each other's eyes. SNOOTY pulls away.]

ALEXIS: You still want me.

SNOOTY: Not anymore.

ALEXIS: You're afraid of me because I understand your world. Too well.

SNOOTY: You don't belong here. Go back home.

ALEXIS: Is that why you wanted to talk to me?

SNOOTY: Yeah. (*ALEXIS flings away her cigarette.*) What?

[ALEXIS suddenly pulls SNOOTY to herself and kisses him on the lips. SNOOTY resists at first but soon succumbs.]

ALEXIS: Marry me.

SNOOTY: Hey. What's the rush?

ALEXIS: I don't like competing with Ellie.

SNOOTY: She's a good friend.

ALEXIS: That's all?

SNOOTY: Yeah. What about Brute? You dealin' with him or what?

ALEXIS: What made you think I'd do business with anyone? (*Beat.*) Brute is Brute, okay?
SNOOTY: And Snooty is Snooty, right?

[Lights and set change to the classroom. MICHAEL returns to his desk as BRUNO threatens with his fists. ELAINE gives BRUNO an "Oh-please" look. While GRAHAM turns to write on the blackboard, BRUNO stands up and towers over ELAINE. BRUNO gestures how "lousy" ELAINE's breasts are. (MICHAEL does not voice himself here.)]

MICHAEL: Hey. You don't talk to girls that way.
BRUNO: Nobody likes you. Mikey, where's your sissy fists?
MICHAEL: Where's your sissy mind?
BRUNO: I'm not sissy. You are.
MICHAEL: Show some respect. One day you will have to.
BRUNO: Never.
MICHAEL: You never learn, do you?
BRUNO: You got that right. For once.

[MICHAEL suddenly punches BRUNO in the stomach. BRUNO collapses. GRAHAM whirls around.]

GRAHAM: Hey.
MICHAEL: I got him, I got him, I got him!
GRAHAM: It's not something to be proud of. Michael, I'll be calling your mother about this.
MICHAEL: I thought you liked me.
GRAHAM: I do. But I can't let you get away with bad things. (*To BRUNO.*) I'm taking you to the infirmary.

[GRAHAM and BRUNO go offstage. OTHERS glance back with admiration at MICHAEL.]

PHIL: That was great!
ELAINE: (*Beat; to MICHAEL.*) Thank you.
MICHAEL: (*Embarrassed.*) You're welcome.

[OTHERS pat MICHAEL on the back. GRAHAM returns to the classroom with both BRUNO and COPP.]

COPP: (*Addresses OTHERS.*) I'd like to talk to everyone for a few minutes. (*To GRAHAM.*) Aren't you going to help me out a little?

GRAHAM: Why don't you try passing Sign Language 101 sometime?

COPP: I don't have the time, all right?

[*OTHERS, trying to lipread, watch this with confusion.*]

GRAHAM: Your students will never understand you. Period.

COPP: Please. (*Clears his throat and faces the class as GRAHAM interprets in SEE.*) I've been thinking a lot about what's happened today, and that's why I wanted to talk to you. (*Looks at BRUNO and MICHAEL.*) You better learn how to talk things out. Work out your differences. You're big boys, not boxers.

[*BRUNO and MICHAEL nod listlessly.*]

COPP: I don't want to keep you from your studies, but I did want all of you to know that if, for any reason, you need help, you should feel free to come to either Ms. Graham or myself. (*To GRAHAM.*) Uh, thank you.

GRAHAM: You're welcome. (*COPP exits; to OTHERS.*) Now do you have any questions before you start your homework?

[*ELAINE raises her hand.*]

GRAHAM: Yes, Elaine?

ELAINE: It's just a history question. Did any of those gangsters from the 1920s ever get married?

[*Lights and set change as "The Wedding March" suddenly comes on. As PRIEST strides up to the pulpit, SNOOTY is standing by himself as OTHERS, except BRUTE, line up facing each other and holding up imaginary rifles skyward, as soldiers might at a military wedding. ELLIE watches all of this from behind the wedding party. ALEXIS, holding an imaginary bouquet of flowers and wearing an imaginary veil, walks slowly under the canopy of rifles held above her head to SNOOTY. When ALEXIS stands next to SNOOTY at last, PRIEST then turns to OTHERS.*]

PRIEST: One final call: Should Mr. Snooty Zook and Ms. Alexis Orlansky not marry? If not, speak now or forever hold your peace.

[ELLIE storms in, breaking ALEXIS and SNOOTY apart.]

SNOOTY: Won't she ever give up?
ELLIE: (To PRIEST.) I do. Look at Alexis's dress.

[ALEXIS looks about herself. Nothing seems to be out of order.]

SNOOTY: She's beautiful. What's the big deal?
ELLIE: You got better eyes than that.
SNOOTY: Let me look. (Pulls out a pair of glasses.) My X-ray glasses.
ALEXIS: (Covers herself.) That's very rude.
SNOOTY: Ellie's got a good point there. (SNOOTY pulls out a gun from inside ALEXIS's outfit.) You? You the one who shot Poppa down?
ALEXIS: What do you think?
SNOOTY: I ain't marryin' you.
ALEXIS: I also have a code of honor, you know.
SNOOTY: Liar.
ALEXIS: Why did you think I came back after all these years? No one's going to save you from me.
SNOOTY: Oh, really?

[ALEXIS lunges forward for her gun, and SNOOTY and ALEXIS struggle for control. ALEXIS finally pries the gun away from him.]

ALEXIS: I belong to no one except my family! (Aims the gun at SNOOTY.) I want to stop you from controlling this town. You took it all away from my father, from my family.
SNOOTY: Go look for a new town to conquer. That'll be more fun.
ALEXIS: No. This is part of my world, too.

[SNOOTY snatches the gun brutally from ALEXIS.]

SNOOTY: If you don't move, I'll shoot ya.

ALEXIS: If you shoot me, you'll have my entire family after yours. Then we'll both be finished.

SNOOTY: Fine.

ALEXIS: You're stubborn, aren't you?

SNOOTY: Go.

ALEXIS: Come on. Shoot me.

[SNOOTY suddenly beckons FIDO over and pulls his hand out. SNOOTY unloads all the bullets from his gun onto FIDO's palm. Done, SNOOTY picks out only one bullet and inserts it into the barrel. Then he spins the barrel.]

ALEXIS: Ha ha.

[SNOOTY aims it at ALEXIS's head.]

SNOOTY: One shot. If no bullet, you must leave this town within one hour. If you get the bullet, you ain't goin' nowhere.

[While SNOOTY and ALEXIS freeze their positions, the set slowly begins to change back to the classroom. Finally, SNOOTY looks about himself and then realizes the absurdity of his gun. He tosses it over his shoulder, and as he becomes MICHAEL and sits in his desk, lights change at last to the classroom. GRAHAM then looks up at an imaginary clock; OTHERS have been doing their homework in this "quiet" time.]

GRAHAM: Oh! It's 2:30 already.

[OTHERS look up at GRAHAM and some of them place their homework on her desk. GRAHAM hears someone knocking. It is COPP again.]

GRAHAM: Excuse me.

[GRAHAM opens the door and confers silently with COPP; she returns as COPP exits.]

GRAHAM: Excuse me, everyone. I want to tell you some good news. A new student will be starting with us tomorrow. Her name is Veronica.

BRUNO: (*Whispers to ANDREW.*) Bet she'll be snooty, too.

[*MICHAEL catches this. The dismissal bell rings.*]

GRAHAM: Oh! Everyone can go home now.

[*OTHERS say "Good-bye, Ms. Graham" and exit. MICHAEL is the last to bid her farewell. He steps out of the classroom and then looks up at the audience.*]

MICHAEL: A new student? Nobody's snooty. Not ever again!

[*MICHAEL exits just as lights BLACKOUT.*]

Love in My Veins

FOR SUSAN JACKSON

DENNIS DRAPER DIRECTED THE world premiere production of *Love in My Veins,* presented by the Illuminations Theater with the Deaf, at Talento Bilingue de Houston, Houston, with the following cast on 6 December 2003.

MINDY: Susan Jackson
HUGH: Scott Hutchison

Susan Jackson was voiced by Rita Aguilar and Scott Hutchison. Jill Beebout and Susan Jackson were the producers.

STAGING CONSIDERATIONS

Both characters are deaf and use ASL to communicate. They can be voiced by two hearing actors for the signing-impaired. Over the course of their twenty-five-year relationship, which travels from the year 1975 to the present, both characters will age from their early twenties to their early fifties. They can wear the same black outfit from beginning to end, with possible clothing accouterments to indicate the fashion of that year.

The following props would be most useful: A loveseat (which can double as car seats), a pair of chairs, and a table.

It may help the audience if the year for each scene was projected on the wall above the actors at the beginning of each scene. This will help convey the years rolling by. Lights can fade in and out between scenes.

ACT ONE
Scene 1: 1975

[Lights suggest a hotel lobby. HUGH sits on a loveseat while watching for a particular person to come through the door. When MINDY enters, a light on her face goes on.]

MINDY: (*To the audience.*) I liked none of the deaf men I knew growing up, so I thought I'd try my luck with hearing men. To each personal ad that I liked, I told each man that I was deaf upfront. No one responded except for Hugh, who was in town for a few months doing research at the University of Houston. He said that should not be a problem and that we should meet anyway.

[HUGH stands up and approaches MINDY.]

HUGH: (*Speaks and gestures.*) Hello?

[MINDY stops when she notices the hearing aids in HUGH's ears.]

MINDY: (*Gestures.*) You deaf? You sign? Why didn't you tell me?
HUGH: (*Not quite understanding her; speaks and gestures.*) I'm Hugh Marvin.
MINDY: (*Gestures.*) What?

[HUGH takes out a small notepad and pen, and scribbles something. Meanwhile MINDY signs to the audience as she reads what he's writing.]

MINDY: "I don't know sign language, but I would like to learn."

[MINDY turns to HUGH and smiles as she gestures that he turn off his voice and take out his hearing aids. HUGH stops. Then he softens as he closes his lips, takes out his hearing aids, and puts them into his pockets. MINDY beams.

Lights change as if they are in a small classroom. MINDY stands before HUGH, sitting on a chair. He is now learning signs.]

MINDY: "Sky."

[*MINDY gestures the sun beating down as the clouds roll across the sky.*]

HUGH: Sky.
MINDY: "Water."

[*MINDY gestures the tidal waves rising up and down, and then the thunderous waters as in the middle of a storm on the sea.*]

HUGH: Water.
MINDY: "Kiss."

[*MINDY gestures a pair of lovers French-kissing, which ends with her arms encircling herself. HUGH hesitates, but he stands up and approaches her.*]

HUGH: Kiss.

[*HUGH looks at the sign he's just made and gestures "Bleech!" He points to his own lips and then to her lips. He leans forward with puckered lips. She laughs. As she joins him in a kiss, lights black out quickly and come back on.*

HUGH and MINDY jump apart from each other, as if caught. They do not interrupt each other, but rather, their lines flow into each other's. They are now at their own mother's houses.]

HUGH: (*Speaks and tries to sign.*) Mom? Guess what?
MINDY: Mom? Guess what?
HUGH: (*Speaks and tries to sign.*) There's nothing wrong with my hands.
MINDY: I met a really nice deaf man.
HUGH: Mom. Don't give me a look like that!
MINDY: He's not from a deaf family like us.
HUGH: All my life I felt like a freak.
MINDY: He's different. Which is what I like.
HUGH: No, Mom, I'm not "normal." I'm *deaf.*
MINDY: Mom! I prefer to marry into a hearing family.
HUGH: For the first time in my life I feel normal.
MINDY: Yes, he's an oralist but he's picking up signs so fast.
HUGH: A woman wants me because I'm deaf.
MINDY: Why do you care? Grandpa was an oralist once.

HUGH: Mom? She's deaf. (*Beat.*) She can't speak.

MINDY: He's a smart man. College-educated. He didn't even go to Gallaudet College.

HUGH: Mom! I love her. Why can't you be happy?

MINDY: When you meet him, don't judge him with your looks.

HUGH: Oh, I realize something now: I'm not a person to you.

MINDY: He's different from the other deaf men I've dated.

HUGH: Mom, I am just this mouth and throat and ears. That's it.

[As MINDY scampers off, HUGH gives chase as slides of water cross-dissolve to a bright light. It is now an early summer evening. HUGH scurries after MINDY as on a beach off Padre Island. He wraps his arms around her waist; she giggles. He smiles.]

MINDY: Look at the skies. The best thing about Texas.

[They scan the skies. He turns her around and looks into her eyes.]

HUGH: You make me feel big as the skies.

MINDY: Big down there, too?

[HUGH blushes. MINDY giggles.]

MINDY: I love your red face. You're so cute. I'll have to embarrass you more often.

[HUGH looks away sheepishly. MINDY glances around.]

MINDY: Look. No one's here.

HUGH: (*Glances around.*) What?

MINDY: (*Coyly.*) Think we could play here? No one drives all the way west on Padre on a weekday. Not in September anyway.

HUGH: Oh, no, no. Someone's bound to catch us.

MINDY: Hugh! From here I can see the faint glimmer of sunset waving good-bye. (*Turns to him.*) We've wasted a most wonderful day on Padre. The last day of our secret engagement.

[HUGH kisses MINDY on the lips.]

HUGH: Now the rest of the world will know about us.

[MINDY seems hesitant.]

HUGH: Something wrong?

MINDY: I'm just worried about how the deaf community will look at you.

HUGH: Why is that such an issue with you? I've never met any of your deaf friends.

[MINDY sighs.]

MINDY: Just that you're interested in me makes me feel good.

HUGH: Just "good"?

MINDY: Most deaf guys aren't as smart as you.

HUGH: Just because I know a lot about statistics and research doesn't mean I'm smart.

MINDY: You know what I meant. I'm only a legal word processor in downtown Houston. Compared to you, I'm nothing.

HUGH: Oh, don't be silly. I love you, remember?

[MINDY stands still as if frozen by time as HUGH turns to the audience.]

HUGH: My parents were professors at Iowa State University, and you'd think they'd be more accepting of a child like me. But no, it was all about pronouncing words and phrases around the dinner table. Every time I ate with my parents, it felt like a speech lesson. (*Beat.*) I remember this girl who lived two doors down from us. No one wanted to play with her because she was in a wheelchair. She wasn't also very bright, but I remember her as the best friend I ever had. She didn't care if I could speak or not. She somehow knew that perfection wasn't everything in life.

[In turn, HUGH stands still as if frozen by time as MINDY turns to the audience.]

MINDY: You stood there and posed for silly pictures with my cheap camera, and I ran through the waves while you took off your shoes and socks, and you had to put them in the right place before you rolled up your pants before running out to meet me. I pulled you down into the waves, and for a minute there you looked so angry that I had to laugh at how soaked you were. You were no longer a textbook, I was no longer just a high school graduate, and we were no longer afraid to kiss.

[MINDY turns to HUGH as lights fade.]

Scene 2: 1978

[HUGH is driving their car (via their loveseat). MINDY is putting on makeup by using an imaginary dashboard mirror. They ride over an occasional bump on the road. Lights up on them from below the dashboard.]

HUGH: I still find it so hard to believe.

MINDY: What?

HUGH: That if we had a hearing baby, everyone would reject us.

MINDY: I swear to you! It's happened to a few of my friends.

HUGH: Then they can't be your friends.

MINDY: They're people I've known all my life.

HUGH: But they can change. What if they have hearing kids?

MINDY: They're out too.

HUGH: Wait. I'm from Iowa; I'm not from around here. You are.

MINDY: That's right. (*Smiles.*) Once a Houston girl, always a Houston girl.

HUGH: People may think I'm just following you like a lovesick puppy.

MINDY: Aren't you? You moved all the way from Iowa to be here with me.

HUGH: The weather here is better.

MINDY: Not much.

[HUGH continues driving. MINDY puts away her makeup kit in her purse. She glances at him.]

MINDY: Something wrong?

[HUGH says nothing.]

MINDY: If you don't want to go to this party, we don't have to go. We can turn around and go right back home.

HUGH: No. We will go. (*Checks watch.*) We're only fifteen minutes away.

MINDY: Then what's bugging you?

[*HUGH glances up in the rearview mirror, drives the car over, and parks on the side of the road.*]

HUGH: You know those friends of yours who got hearing babies?

MINDY: (*Nods.*) What?

HUGH: Don't you ever visit them?

MINDY: I don't want the deaf community to catch me.

HUGH: Is being hearing that horrible?

MINDY: It is to the deaf community here.

HUGH: What if we happened to have a hearing baby?

MINDY: They would not accept us.

HUGH: Then how could they be friends? They're people you see at deaf events and parties all the time.

MINDY: You don't understand.

HUGH: I do understand something about rejection. I've been rejected all my life. You've never been rejected? Whoo-oo!

MINDY: Stop mocking me.

HUGH: (*Stops.*) I'm sorry. Just that I find it so hard to believe anyone would reject us for having a hearing baby.

MINDY: That's why I don't want kids. Too much of a risk.

HUGH: I'd prefer a deaf baby, too, but if it happens to be hearing, that's fine too.

MINDY: I can't risk losing my friends.

HUGH: Then tell me what "friends" mean.

MINDY: Stop questioning me. This is not a courtroom.

HUGH: If you're letting friends stop you from getting what you want, then they can't be your friends. That's what it looks like to me.

MINDY: Should I lie to everyone that I can't have babies?

[*HUGH looks about himself.*]

HUGH: We should have one child. Just one. I want to be a better parent than my own parents were.

MINDY: But you have no family now. Just me and my huge deaf family.

HUGH: They don't seem to like me much anyway.

MINDY: Give them time. They'll come around.

HUGH: How many years must I wait for their approval? I *married* you, for God's sake! I feel they're mocking me, sometimes. I'm not deaf enough, I'm not—

[MINDY brings her hands to his and soothes them.]

MINDY: You have to give the deaf community time. They're giving you time, you know. Strangers have come in and tried to force speech on them or make them feel like nothing. We're all strangers to each other, and they need to see that you're serious about living in Houston.

HUGH: I've been here for three years. Why can't being deaf be enough to get accepted! What more do they want from me?

MINDY: Oh, they'll accept you. They know you're number one in my life. They've known me all their lives and it's hard for them to imagine me falling for someone like you. But I have.

HUGH: "Someone like me"? Were you supposed to fall for some high school dropout? Are you supposed to answer to those kinds of expectations from the deaf community?

MINDY: No. You know.

HUGH: Fine.

[HUGH restarts the engine. MINDY taps on his shoulder.]

MINDY: No, it's not fine.

HUGH: You're so used to having everything happen your way.

MINDY: We can move to Iowa if you like it there better.

HUGH: No. My job's good. The hospital's expanding. I have a very good chance of moving up the ladder there, run my department, and have a say in what we need to research.

MINDY: Fine. But I warn you, you can't look back on this night and wish we'd done things differently. You can't change the past.

HUGH: (*Beat.*) What kind of future did you hope for when you married me?

MINDY: A social life. Something you never had.

HUGH: How about a family I've never had?

MINDY: We can talk some more about this after the party.

HUGH: Right.

[*HUGH glances back before pressing the gas pedal and sliding back onto the highway.*]

Scene 3: 1981

[*HUGH closes the front door on stage right. MINDY is sitting, exhausted on the living room sofa. HUGH returns to MINDY.*]

MINDY: That boy is nice, but I'm so happy we don't have kids!

HUGH: He wasn't so bad. Hearing, yes, but he sure can sign.

MINDY: He was running around. Crazy! I thought he was going to knock over that vase.

HUGH: He's only six years old.

MINDY: But look at what his parents had to go through.

HUGH: I think they're really nice people. I'm glad we're good friends with them.

[*MINDY says nothing.*]

HUGH: Oh, I see. You're worried that if word gets out that we've allowed the Yerkers and their *hearing* children over to our house, we'll be excommunicated from the House of Deaf Community?

MINDY: Oh, God, no. Not again.

HUGH: Why?

MINDY: (*Beat.*) Why did you marry me if you want kids so much?

HUGH: Maybe it sounds stupid, but I thought love could change everything.

MINDY: Love never changes. It just amplifies everything.

HUGH: What's so horrible about kids, anyway?

MINDY: It's too much work. We'd never have a social life.

HUGH: We don't have much of a social life anyway.

MINDY: That's because you don't like half of the people here. I just wish you'd focus on liking the other half.

HUGH: My job, you know? I work very hard. I'm proud that I made it to Assistant Head of the department. I'm the most important deaf person in the hospital now.

MINDY: They don't care about that. They care whether you're a good and honest person. You need to show that part of yourself to them more often.

HUGH: And get rejected for trying? Sometimes I wonder why I moved down here. I thought Texans were the friendliest people in the country.

MINDY: They are. (*Pats on the sofa next to her.*) Come here.

[*HUGH sits down next to her.*]

MINDY: You didn't move here because of the great blue skies. You moved here because of me.

HUGH: But you're not enough.

MINDY: Not one person can ever be everything for anyone. We all have to make compromises sometime.

HUGH: We don't have to compromise. I want a child. Let's have our own world where it's just the three of us. You, me, and our child. Hey, we can invite deaf parents with hearing kids over.

MINDY: Sounds nice. But I don't want to give up my deaf friends.

HUGH: Now you know why I don't go out as much as you do. They put up with me because I married you, not because they like me.

MINDY: I grew up in their world. We all went to the same deaf school so we're like a family. We have a shared history.

HUGH: (*Struck with a new idea.*) What if we adopted a deaf child? You know, from China?

MINDY: Adopt?

HUGH: You're afraid of giving birth to a hearing baby anyway.

MINDY: Why are you so obsessed with children?

HUGH: Because I want to be a father! Ten years from now those friends of yours who still go down to the deaf club are going to look like sad cases because they don't have kids who love them.

MINDY: Kids aren't everything. We're just different. We're not like any other deaf couple we know.

HUGH: Except Rex and James.

MINDY: They're, uhm, an exception, but they seem to be doing okay here. They don't go to the deaf club at all.

HUGH: I don't like them. They're [*gay*] disgusting.

MINDY: We can be strong like them. We can be very honest and say: "We don't want children."

HUGH: They're never going to accept us for that. They'll think we're both gay.

MINDY: They probably thought that after the first year. (*Beat.*) Let them talk.

HUGH: They better not think I'm gay. I'm a man!

MINDY: Oh, *that* I already know. Always horny.

HUGH: I can't help it if you make me hard.

[*MINDY smiles.*]

HUGH: What?

MINDY: I think we're out of condoms.

HUGH: Shit.

MINDY: I can go get some if you like.

HUGH: No, I'll go.

[*HUGH stands up.*]

MINDY: We don't have to do it right now.

HUGH: Why? You can't keep up like this—always hot one minute, always cold the next. That drives me crazy.

MINDY: Sex should be spontaneous. It shouldn't be like a doctor's appointment.

HUGH: Very funny.

MINDY: It's true. If we had to have the same meal every day, I'd die of boredom. But if I know there's going to be something different on the plate, I'd be more hungry than you think.

HUGH: So what you're telling me is that I'm the same meal every day.

[MINDY says nothing.]

HUGH: You're dying of boredom every night, is that it?

[MINDY says nothing.]

HUGH: Answer me!

MINDY: I didn't say that.

HUGH: I want you to be hungry for me as I am for you. Isn't that why we got married?

MINDY: (Beat.) Yes.

HUGH: Then we don't need condoms. That'd be something different. More like dessert, maybe?

[MINDY glances away, then gets up.]

MINDY: I'll go get the condoms.

HUGH: No. *I'll* get them.

MINDY: You don't have the guts to—

HUGH: Why do you have to mock me? I work hard with my numbers and reports—50 hours a week—and you think I can't handle a simple shopping trip to the drugstore and ask for some condoms? You really insult me.

[HUGH leaves. MINDY sits down and sighs.]

Scene 4: 1986

[HUGH, having come home from work, enters and sits on the loveseat. MINDY enters.]

MINDY: Home late again.

[They peck each other on the lips.]

HUGH: Yeah. A lot of reports had to be finished by tomorrow.

[MINDY *sits next to her husband.*]

MINDY: Maybe you should think about changing jobs or something. I almost never see you anymore.

HUGH: Why? I'm the department head now.

MINDY: I want to talk to you about something.

HUGH: What?

MINDY: I'm thinking of going to college.

HUGH: That's so great! What are you thinking of studying?

MINDY: I think I want to teach computers. Maybe community college level or something. I'm just so tired of word processing!

[HUGH *nods.*]

MINDY: I'm thinking of quitting my job for school.

HUGH: Fine. Why not leave your job two weeks before you go to school? That way you can still work and keep saving up more money.

MINDY: You make plenty of money now.

HUGH: We don't have wealthy parents, so we have to save up. You never know.

MINDY: We never spend any of that money. All we do is save, save, and save. And then what?

HUGH: We will spend when we retire. That's what we agreed on.

MINDY: I know. But I know that we have more money than any of our friends.

HUGH: You told everyone how much we have in the bank?

MINDY: I never told anyone.

HUGH: Good. It's no one's business.

MINDY: Why can't we do something different? Be like them.

HUGH: Meaning?

MINDY: We should go to the ASL Social on Friday night. See our old friends and catch up with them.

HUGH: Why? What for?

MINDY: I sit all day in my lawyer's office. No one around me signs. I'm just another nice deaf person who can type 120 words a minute, and they all smile at me because they don't know how to communicate or they don't care to try! I'm sick and tired of being lonely over there. I'm a person! I'm just like them. I'm much more than just these fast fingers!

[HUGH pulls MINDY into a hug of comfort. She moves back a bit to communicate.]

MINDY: That's why I have to go out and be with deaf people all the time. Chatting with them makes me feel better.

HUGH: Can't I make you feel better?

MINDY: You do. But you know.

HUGH: No, I don't.

MINDY: I feel great when I can sign. Don't you remember how it felt to you when you began learning signs?

HUGH: (Smiles.) Yeah. Remember this?

[HUGH makes the sign for "kiss" and makes the gesture for "bleech" as in Act I, Scene 1. MINDY laughs.]

MINDY: I'd forgotten!

HUGH: How can I forget anything as beautiful as you? (Caresses MINDY's chin.) You are my world. I don't care what our mothers say about us.

MINDY: I still find it funny that both our mothers have never met. And we've been married for almost ten years!

HUGH: Sometimes I think families hurt more than help.

MINDY: I hate it sometimes when some people come up to me at deaf events and say, "Your mother wants to know why you don't have kids yet." The nerve!

HUGH: I thought you'd be used to this by now. Seems not.

MINDY: I just hide it whenever I go out.

HUGH: You hide a lot of things. That's not good for you.

MINDY: What else am I supposed to do?

HUGH: We could have a social life limited to just a few friends, and not worry about the gossiping and backstabbing out there.

MINDY: But I love mingling with deaf people.

HUGH: Well, it's up to you.

MINDY: As long as we stay away from our families, we'll be fine.

HUGH: You know what? Let's go upstairs to bed.

MINDY: You're different from the other deaf men I know. We've been together for ten years and you're still horny for me. I hear so many friends having affairs all the time, and I can't believe it hasn't happened to us.

HUGH: Do you want it to happen to us?

MINDY: No! (*Beat.*) I feel so lucky.

HUGH: You should. I'm the one who wants you. All of you.

MINDY: (*Trying to be coy.*) Really?

HUGH: Of course! Look at you. You're beautiful!

[*MINDY smiles. HUGH stands up.*]

HUGH: Let's go upstairs.

MINDY: Why not stay here and have fun?

HUGH: That's really fine.

[*HUGH beams and cradles her in his arms for what promises to be a hot kiss. Lights black out.*]

Scene 5: 1987

[*They come home from an evening party. HUGH sits down on the sofa and turns on the TV.*]

MINDY: Why are you watching TV so late?

HUGH: The party was boring so I thought I should watch something different for a few minutes.

MINDY: I see.

[*MINDY sits down next to HUGH.*]

MINDY: What was so boring about the party? Lots of deaf people there.

HUGH: Oh, the same old, same old.

MINDY: Nothing wrong with that.
HUGH: Yeah, right. (*Watches something.*)

[MINDY touches HUGH's arm.]

HUGH: What!
MINDY: Sorry.

[MINDY gets up. HUGH notices this.]

HUGH: Did you have something you wanted to tell me?

[MINDY pauses.]

MINDY: Actually, yes.
HUGH: Go on.

[MINDY takes HUGH's TV remote and shuts it off.]

HUGH: Why did you do that for?
MINDY: I have to tell you something important.
HUGH: What?
MINDY: I'm pregnant.

[HUGH stops.]

HUGH: Wait a minute—what happened? Pregnant? How many
    months? (*Touches her stomach.*) We haven't fucked in. . . .
MINDY: That's right.
HUGH: (*Beat.*) It's not mine.

[MINDY says nothing.]

HUGH: (*More as an accusation than a question.*) How could you?
MINDY: Accident.
HUGH: But you were so careful not to want my baby. (*Beat.*)
    That's it.
MINDY: What?
HUGH: Here's what we're going to do. We'll never share the same
    bed ever again—
MINDY: I'm not keeping the baby.

HUGH: I don't care. I'll file for a divorce anyway.

MINDY: It was an accident!

HUGH: Dennis, huh?

MINDY: (*Beat.*) It just happened.

HUGH: Does his wife know?

MINDY: No.

HUGH: Does *he* know?

MINDY: No. He doesn't want to leave his wife. (*Beat.*) He's so in love with being a father, taking his son everywhere.

HUGH: Fatherhood can really change a man. I wonder if motherhood will change you.

MINDY: I'm not that cold-hearted!

HUGH: You don't want my children, but yet you allow someone else to make a baby inside you. How do you think that makes me feel?

[MINDY reaches out to touch HUGH, but he brushes her off. He is about to storm off but changes his mind.]

HUGH: I forgot to tell you something else. You know that new hearing co-worker named Nina Keyes? Short with blue glasses, and always trying to sign? She works as my department secretary. She wanted to sleep with me once, but I said, No, let's keep things professional. But you know what? She's not married, and she's been talking about getting impregnated anyway so she can have a child of her own to raise. She always complained that all the good men are married or gay. Well, she can take me!

[HUGH storms off as lights fade.]

Scene 6: 1988

[To the sound effect of the gavel, lights open on HUGH and MINDY facing the audience if they are their new unseen lovers. Their lines should almost blend into each other.]

MINDY: My new man.

HUGH: My new woman.

MINDY: You look at me with new eyes.

HUGH: You look at me as a real man.

MINDY: You make me feel more like a woman I never thought possible.

HUGH: You let me do anything I want, and without shame.

MINDY: I never knew my own body could be so filled with intense pleasure, and you found all the treasure spots and kissed X's all over them. We hid our secrets all over each other's bodies, and threw away the maps.

HUGH: Sweat watered the garden of earthly pleasures, and each time I weeded your body with the fork of my tongue, you bloomed even more. I never knew I could feel so clean.

MINDY: You look at me with new eyes.

HUGH: You look at me as a real man.

MINDY: You treat me differently, as if I am a precious black pearl found in the shore.

HUGH: You make me feel proud of my own body, begging for another round of gardening.

MINDY: Each time you kiss me . . .

HUGH: Each time you kiss me . . .

MINDY: . . . my black pearl turns white as the sun beating down on our bodies as we dive into the ocean of each other.

HUGH: . . . I am forevermore lost in the morning dew of a summer dream.

[Lights fade, then blink on to the sound effect of a gavel pounding as HUGH and MINDY jump further apart from each other and face the audience as if on trial.]

HUGH: Your Honor . . .

MINDY: I wish to present the case of . . .

HUGH: Marvin versus Marvin.

MINDY: My client pleads . . .

HUGH: Not guilty.

MINDY: *Not* guilty.

HUGH: Your Honor . . .

MINDY: It was an accident.

HUGH: Circumstantial evidence!

MINDY: Our eyes bumped into each other.

HUGH: Two of a kind.

MINDY: He was deaf.

HUGH: She was hearing. Learning to sign.

MINDY: He was married.

HUGH: Mine wasn't.

MINDY: His deaf wife just had a baby. A deaf baby! She had no idea how lucky she was.

HUGH: She was a lonely department secretary. Worked too many hours like I did.

MINDY: He was absolutely terrified of being a father. And she didn't want him anymore.

HUGH: Your Honor, I wish to plead.

MINDY: (*Turns to HUGH.*) Guilty!

HUGH: (*Turns to MINDY.*) Who are you to judge me? You're guilty too!

MINDY: (*Returns to the audience.*) Your Honor, I seek a sensible sentence . . .

HUGH: How do you wish to atone? (*Turns to MINDY.*) Bitch.

MINDY: (*Tries to ignore his comment.*) That would somehow repay my huge debt to society.

HUGH: *Deaf* society! You don't mess around with other people's marriages.

MINDY: I never intended to be a homewrecker.

HUGH: Your Honor, I'd like to ask for a far stricter sentence against Dennis Jones. He should be castrated.

MINDY: (*To HUGH.*) You can't speak for him. He's different from you.

HUGH: I can. Because you married me, not him!

MINDY: (*Beat.*) I know. (*Beat.*) He went back to her.

HUGH: I fired Nina.

MINDY: Why?

HUGH: She seemed to undress me with her eyes all the time. Plus I didn't want to lose my standing at the hospital.

MINDY: (*Tries not to laugh.*) Undress you with her eyes? (*Looks all over him.*) I've seen you naked a hundred times.

HUGH: (*Bitterly.*) If that.

[*Lights change. HUGH and MINDY acknowledge each other with a slight nod before returning to sit together on the living room sofa. They both hesitate in looking at each other.*]

MINDY: (*Finally.*) I'm sorry.

HUGH: I'm sorry too.

MINDY: I have terrible taste in men.

HUGH: I know.

MINDY: Are you seeing anyone now?

[*HUGH shakes his head no. MINDY nods quietly.*]

HUGH: Some women still think I'm gay. But you know what? I'm okay with it. A lot of women have this fantasy of making a gay guy go straight, so if that's what it takes to get them into my bed, I'm fine with it.

MINDY: You—you sleep with them?

HUGH: Some.

MINDY: Anyone I know?

HUGH: You said that jealousy's the worst thing for any relationship.

MINDY: Right.

HUGH: Your boxes are in the garage.

MINDY: I noticed. I didn't realize I had so much stuff. You didn't have to pack them. That wasn't part of our divorce agreement.

HUGH: It's okay. I had to do something when I wasn't dating or working.

[*MINDY looks about, keeping her face away from his, and somehow— suddenly—their hands fly together in a firm clasp. They still refuse to look at each other.*]

Scene 7: 1990

[MINDY turns off an imaginary showerhead, wraps a towel around herself, and steps out of the shower while HUGH lathers imaginary shaving cream all over his jaw and starts shaving. He notices her in the bathroom mirror.]

HUGH: Good morning, beautiful!
MINDY: Good morning.
HUGH: Sleep well?

[MINDY nods as she takes a smaller towel from a rack and starts drying her hair.]

MINDY: You too?

[HUGH nods. He smiles and kisses her on the nose. She flinches when she finds a dab of shaving cream on her nose.]

HUGH: Now I have to shave your nose.
MINDY: I don't have a hairy nose!

[HUGH laughs.]

MINDY: I haven't seen you laugh in such a long time.
HUGH: It's so good to be with you again. Even though we've divorced. (*Beat.*) I mean, I saw you so clearly last night without all the bullshit, and you were still so beautiful. Why did we have to let all that get in the way before?
MINDY: Foolishness? (*Stops.*) What will our friends think? I hope they didn't see my car parked in front of your house.
HUGH: I don't care what they think. Let them think we're Elizabeth Taylor and Richard Burton.
MINDY: But they couldn't stay together.
HUGH: They were really in love with love. That's all.
MINDY: That's all? Sometimes I wonder.
HUGH: Wonder what?
MINDY: Sometimes I think they got back together because they were lonely. Like us.

HUGH: You make us sound like a pair of two lonely old people. We're not old.

MINDY: Look at me. (*Opens her imaginary towel to reveal her body.*) I'm not the same woman you fell for fifteen years ago.

HUGH: Neither am I. But I'm okay with it. I wouldn't want to have the same body all the time. Change is a good thing.

MINDY: I don't want to grow old and ugly.

[*HUGH turns to MINDY.*]

MINDY: What?

HUGH: I wanted you, and I slept with you last night! What's the matter with you?

MINDY: I don't know. I just keep thinking there's got to be more to life than this.

HUGH: I would've been fine with you. Except. . . .

MINDY: I'm sorry, sorry, sorry! All right?

HUGH: You don't have to apologize anymore. It's all in the past.

MINDY: Maybe we should call in sick and drive out to Padre Island.

HUGH: (*Smiles.*) That's so funny. I was there just last week. Sometimes I spend hours sitting right at the edge of the shore where the waves come right up to me. But I never get wet. Sometimes I touch the water, and then it feels cold. Like I always did whenever you went away.

MINDY: Oh, Hugh. I'm such a stupid girl.

HUGH: No, you're not. For two reasons: You are not stupid. And you are not a girl. You're a *woman*. Just the way I like it.

MINDY: You're too good for me.

HUGH: Nonsense.

MINDY: I mean it, really. You should look for a better wife than me.

HUGH: We're not getting remarried. That's not a possibility.

MINDY: No one wants me. Well, I shouldn't say that. Deaf divorced men seem very interested in me, but they're not—

HUGH: They're not me. Right?

[MINDY nods.]

HUGH: I've never wanted anyone else. But I have to be realistic. I have to move on.

MINDY: Have you dated anyone I know?

HUGH: Why does it matter who?

MINDY: Deaf culture.

[HUGH rolls his eyes. He has finished shaving and starts wiping his face clean.]

HUGH: That's a very lame excuse to be nosy. Besides, I thought you got over that a long time ago when you got your A.A. degree in Computer Instruction.

MINDY: Just because I work in the hearing world doesn't mean I have to forget deaf culture. We are a blunt people because hearies always like to elaborate with lots of words so no one can understand them. They like to *sound* important.

HUGH: You know that's not true. I read journals too. You just have to learn how to read.

MINDY: I do know how to read!

HUGH: I said "how." If you've studied statistical analysis, you'd question how the study was set up, and whether the study was valid. Most of them are, but you can't just assume that someone with a Ph.D. did the study right. Journals are just a place where we analyze each other, and see how we can improve our research. I've explained all of this to you before.

MINDY: I know, but. . . .

HUGH: You don't need to feel stupid. I didn't want to marry a textbook anyway. I love you. I always have. Even though you've hurt me many times, I still feel love in my veins for you. Every time I see you, I feel a little warm inside. My heart keeps beating with hope that you'll change.

MINDY: I'll change. What do you want me to be?

HUGH: Yourself. I can't expect you to change for me.

MINDY: I'll change. I promise.

HUGH: Don't make promises you can't keep.

MINDY: I do keep promises.

HUGH: Our marriage vows were a promise.

MINDY: I made a mistake, okay? I thought you forgave me.

HUGH: I guess it's too late for us to have a child.

MINDY: I can start fertility drug treatments. Increase my chances of getting pregnant.

HUGH: It's still a bad idea, anyway.

MINDY: We can work it out.

HUGH: No, no. It's okay. (*Checks his watch.*) I gotta go.

MINDY: What about calling in sick? (*Beat.*) Padre Island.

HUGH: I want to, but I can't. I have a big budget meeting with the Head of Finance Department today.

MINDY: I see.

HUGH: Just keep Padre Island warm in your heart. We'll find our way back. You can stay here and then leave when you're ready for the day.

MINDY: Thanks. You're a good man, you know?

[HUGH nods and leaves.]

Scene 8: 1991

[HUGH and MINDY stand facing each other. They are getting remarried.]

HUGH and MINDY: (*Simultaneously.*) "I do."

[They kiss. As they walk down the aisle from the farthest back of the stage, they walk as if in slow-motion but they talk to the imaginary well-wishers in the pews and to the audience in turns. They constantly smile.]

HUGH: (*Nods thanks to a well-wisher; then to the audience.*) How strange that more people have shown up at our second wedding than at our first.

MINDY: (*Nods thanks to a well-wisher; then to the audience.*) Why do I feel like a train wreck trying to pick up speed? I feel as if we're going up a bigger mountain and gravity keeps pulling us backwards.

HUGH: It's a different sort of love.

MINDY: Very different.

HUGH: At least she lets me make love to her.

MINDY: I think I need a partnership. Someone to guide me on the right path.

HUGH: She even lets me take care of her. A consideration if you can't have a child.

MINDY: They're watching our every move. As if they've set up bets to see how long this second marriage will last.

[At that point, lights blink. HUGH pulls up a chair, and MINDY lifts one of her legs onto it. HUGH turns to the imaginary crowd of well-wishers.]

HUGH: You know what they say? Pulling her garter off is going to be even hotter because I know exactly what I'm getting.

MINDY: Oh, stop it! Take it off.

HUGH: I'll take *everything* off.

[MINDY blushes. She smiles as he lifts her imaginary dress and slides down her garter. He holds it up in the air.]

HUGH: Anyone in the mood to get married? (*Beat.*) All the single guys should get in front. Good. I'll turn around and toss it over my head, okay?

[HUGH does so. MINDY stops. He turns to catch the look on her face, then looks at the imaginary winner.]

HUGH: (*Beat.*) Congratulations, Dennis. I didn't know you were single again. (*Beat; tries not to appear too gleeful.*) Separated? Sorry to hear that.

Scene 9: 1994

[HUGH is sitting on the sofa watching TV when MINDY, slightly drunk, enters. She laughs a lot in this scene; she sign-slurs her lines.]

MINDY: Why are you sitting there?

HUGH: Watching *Biography*. Tonight it's about Laurent Clerc.

MINDY: Clerc? He made it to the big time? Whoo-ooo!

HUGH: What's gotten into you?

MINDY: It was a good party. (*Hiccups.*) Oops.

HUGH: Just because you lost your job recently doesn't mean you have to go out there and get drunk. Who knows, your future boss might've been there.

MINDY: I don't care.

HUGH: Sit down.

MINDY: You can't be my big daddy.

HUGH: You're acting like a child right now.

MINDY: Says who? I'm one year older than you.

HUGH: Age is a state of mind. Means nothing.

MINDY: Oh, so you're Mr. Marvin, the ever-responsible clinical researcher who never misses a single payment on any of our bills?

HUGH: It's important to stay out of debt as much as possible so we can have extra money to travel. Which we never do.

MINDY: Oh, where did you want to go this time?

HUGH: I'd like to go to Switzerland.

MINDY: That's so boring. Big mountains, big chocolate, big cheese. Yeah, right.

HUGH: You're not even interested in traveling?

MINDY: Imagine the hours it would take to fly there. *Hours.*

HUGH: What if I wanted to treat you to a trip?

MINDY: Nah. Save your money.

HUGH: For what? We haven't gone anywhere since I moved to Houston.

MINDY: That's not true. What about the NAD conventions?

HUGH: Those don't count. I'm talking about *vacations*. Away from everyone and everything!

MINDY: I gotta go to the bathroom.

HUGH: Go!

[MINDY staggers offstage. HUGH resumes watching the TV and in doing so, he speaks to the TV.]

HUGH: How would *Biography* summarize our messy lives to a hearing America? First, it would show how happy we were as children. Mindy playing in the backyard with her deaf parents north of Houston. Me tagging along after my hearing brothers and parents on interminable road trips all over America. Mindy winning one Popularity Award after another in her deaf high school. Me sitting in the front row of my hearing classes and trying to lipread all those long-syllabic words in Chemistry. Mindy laughing with her deaf friends during her high school graduation. Me trying my best to smile at my own graduation.

[HUGH freezes. MINDY steps into a spotlight behind HUGH.]

MINDY: O the days of being young and wild: How we couldn't stop looking at each other. He was already learning how to sign, and I was amazed that he'd been learning it for a month! How we couldn't stop talking with each other. I was in love with his steady hands, always searching for the precise word, and I was always searching for the precise sign for all his words.

[HUGH stands up into another spotlight.]

HUGH: O the days of being young and wild: I had dated hearing women before, but she was different. My deafness wasn't an issue; in fact, it made me more attractive to her. How odd to think that the one thing that hindered me all my life was the most beautiful thing to her. How we couldn't stop talking with each other. I was in love with never using my voice and finding my own hands far more talkative. It was as if my incessant signing had to make up for the wasted hours around my family's dinner table all these years.

[Spotlights switch to regular lighting as before. HUGH is still standing, but he is turning to MINDY staggering back from the bathroom.]

HUGH: You all right?
MINDY: Yes.

HUGH: You really should sit down.

[MINDY *doesn't argue as she does so; she's a little less drunk. HUGH sits down next to her.*]

HUGH: If you need to see a counselor, my insurance can cover it.
MINDY: No. I'm not an alcoholic.
HUGH: No one will share your secrets with the world.
MINDY: The deaf community knows who I am. What if my deaf counselor already knows who I am?
HUGH: Okay. So you want a hearing counselor and an interpreter. Let's see: That means *two* people will know more of your secrets.
MINDY: You don't understand.
HUGH: I do understand. You think hearies don't gossip and backstab like our friends do. Want the truth? They're no different from us.
MINDY: Doesn't matter.
HUGH: Fine. I'm going to bed, then.
MINDY: Wait. I'm not ready.
HUGH: You're a big girl now.
MINDY: I hate it when you talk to me that way.
HUGH: Then stop acting like a child. I'm sick and tired of you feeling sorry for yourself because you lost your job, your family didn't invite you to your brother's wedding, and you feel lonely because I'm traveling all the time now. Why don't you grow up?
MINDY: I'm all grown up. (*Hiccups.*) I met someone.
HUGH: I see. (*Beat.*) Did you two have a good time?
MINDY: (*Laughs softly.*) It was very clumsy. He lasted only five minutes. (*Beat.*) He was drunk.
HUGH: (*Beat.*) My friends were right. This marriage is a joke.
MINDY: Please.
HUGH: Begging doesn't look good on you. Sleep there [*on the sofa*] tonight.
MINDY: But—but. . . .

[HUGH *has already gone offstage.*]

Scene 10: 1995

[MINDY is standing by the door while HUGH, sitting at his imaginary desk, checks the bills and uses a calculator to doublecheck the amount. She watches him with a tinge of sadness on her face. He seems completely oblivious until he senses something. He turns from his chair and smiles.]

HUGH: There you are!

MINDY: Yeah.

HUGH: I was going to come pick you up at the clinic.

[HUGH stands up and embraces her.]

HUGH: How are you feeling?

MINDY: Okay. Better, anyway.

HUGH: That's good. Could I get you something?

MINDY: Just water. (*Beat.*) No Houston tap water, please.

[HUGH smiles and leaves.]

MINDY: (*To the audience.*) For six months, I sat apart from others in my ward. They were all deaf, most of whom I knew vaguely from my days of growing up at the Texas School of the Deaf. They'd never gone to college, and I felt a little strange around them. They gave me looks that meant that I wasn't one of them, that I should've known better than to check in, now that I had a "rich" husband. (*Beat.*) It was hard to stop wanting one more drink, but I had to look at myself in the mirror. I had to take off my sunglasses. I was old. My dreams were old. I had squandered away so much. How could I have been so blind?

[HUGH returns with a glass of ice water.]

MINDY: Thanks.

HUGH: You're welcome.

MINDY: I'm amazed you haven't left me.

HUGH: I was so proud of you when you asked your mother to come visit you at the clinic.

MINDY: That was so hard. I didn't realize how much I truly hated her until that moment. (*Beat.*) And I had to ask for forgiveness.

HUGH: I know. Part of the recovery process.

MINDY: (*Sighs.*) I'm trying so hard to ask forgiveness. I don't like to beg, you know? (*Beat.*) I can't believe you'd be willing to forgive me after all I've done to you.

HUGH: I still believe in our marriage vows. That I would be there for you, no matter what.

MINDY: No matter what?

HUGH: Yes.

[MINDY sits down on the sofa and sets aside her glass.]

MINDY: Please sit down.

HUGH: (*Apprehensively.*) Okay.

MINDY: I got something to tell you.

HUGH: What now?

MINDY: (*Sighs.*) The clinic ran some tests on my blood. I tested positive for, you know.

HUGH: I don't understand.

MINDY: I made a mistake! Too many mistakes!

HUGH: Yeah, but I'm still here. What are you talking about?

MINDY: I could die!

HUGH: We're all going to die sometime. What's the big deal?

MINDY: You should get tested too.

HUGH: For what?

MINDY: (*Stares at HUGH.*) I'm positive.

HUGH: (*Quietly.*) You got to be joking.

[MINDY shakes her head no.]

HUGH: You demanded that I use a rubber all these years because you didn't want to get pregnant, and then you demanded that I not use a rubber because you weren't sleeping with anyone else but me. Now you've made me pregnant with *your* disease, and I can't have an abortion like you did! Fuck you!

[HUGH storms off. MINDY sits shocked. Lights fade to BLACKOUT.]

END OF ACT ONE.

ACT TWO

Scene 11: 1996

[HUGH *is sitting on the sofa and looks around the living room. MINDY enters, a little distracted.*]

MINDY: You know where I put that Dorothy Miles book?
HUGH: I never knew you liked her work.
MINDY: Always did. Did you put her away with your books?
HUGH: Yes.
MINDY: Then I want it back.
HUGH: Fine. I'll get it for you.
MINDY: Thanks.

[HUGH *gets up and scans the imaginary bookshelf on stage left. He finds the book and hands it to her.*]

MINDY: Thanks. (*Checks the inscription on the title page.*) Look, she wrote it in here—"For anyone lucky enough to find this and be deaf at the same time. Dot." Isn't that cute?

[HUGH *shrugs his shoulders.*]

MINDY: You're still angry.
HUGH: (*Beat.*) When are the movers supposed to arrive?
MINDY: In about thirty minutes.
HUGH: Only thirty minutes? I thought it was later.
MINDY: You disappointed or what?
HUGH: No. I just want to get this over with.
MINDY: You got big plans for your life without me?
HUGH: My plans were never big. Just small and realistic. So I'd never get disappointed.
MINDY: What can I do to help you forgive me?
HUGH: Nothing. Just leave.

[MINDY *walks slowly around the living room.*]

HUGH: Have you finished packing?

MINDY: Pretty much.

HUGH: Good.

MINDY: You know something? I've forgiven you for sleeping with your secretary Nina.

HUGH: Thanks.

MINDY: She thought I was stupid to leave you.

HUGH: How strange. I fired her, and she still thought well of me?

MINDY: She said there wasn't another man like you. Didn't matter whether you were deaf or hearing. But she felt that if a special man like you was deaf, it made you even more unique.

HUGH: Then why were you bored with me before?

MINDY: The past is past. I don't want to go there.

HUGH: You'll keep traveling there until your final days.

MINDY: That's not true. I'll meet a nice man who can accept me as I am, and then I'll be fine.

HUGH: If I ever hear of anyone dating you, I'll be sure to let him know that you're positive. Just to make sure you're not lying and hurting anyone else.

MINDY: I'll never hurt anyone as long as I live. I swear!

HUGH: Then stop hurting me. Stop talking about the meds, the doctors, the T-cell counts—

MINDY: It's your life too.

HUGH: Which *you* gave me. Thank you very much.

MINDY: I'm sorry—

HUGH: You've apologized enough already. I'm stuck with this, and you've decided to move on out to a new city where you've never been. (*Beat.*) But all your years here in Houston will never leave you behind. Someone will know someone who knows about our two marriages. Before you even step into the new deaf community, they'll ask you: "What happened?" What are you going to tell them?

MINDY: I'm not going to answer that question. Ever.

HUGH: Then they'll never accept you as you are. They'll see you're strong-deaf, but beyond that, they'll never trust you.

MINDY: Oh, they will.

HUGH: I can see it so clearly now: Your job. When you finish teaching, you go visit the deaf club and chat. When you finish chatting, you go home to an empty bed. You're going to be very lonely.

MINDY: Stop acting as if you're God, punishing me! I can't stand it!

HUGH: I know you.

MINDY: I know you too.

HUGH: No, you don't.

MINDY: Oh? Like what?

HUGH: I've already set up a date with a new woman. Lauren.

MINDY: (*Shocked.*) Lauren Hollis?

[HUGH *nods.*]

MINDY: How could you?

HUGH: Why not?

MINDY: She's boring.

HUGH: She's safe and responsible. Unlike you.

MINDY: Does she know about you?

HUGH: I'll tell her when the time is right.

MINDY: Oh, like the night before you marry her?

HUGH: I'd never do that to anyone.

MINDY: Oh, there you go: Saint Hugh. The deaf man who managed to get respected by everyone in his community by never offending anyone, *ever*.

HUGH: I'm a little more honest than you.

[MINDY *laughs.*]

HUGH: What's so funny?

MINDY: Nina said you told her that you loved her.

HUGH: That was a long time ago. I made a mistake, okay?

MINDY: She said that you were her "favorite mistake." Very odd phrase, don't you think?

HUGH: Probably a hearing thing.

[HUGH nods slowly. They've run out of things to say. MINDY plops down on the sofa.]

MINDY: Why can't we work this out? Maybe it'd be easier now that we're talking. *Really* talking.

HUGH: We've tried. *Twice.*

MINDY: I screwed up both times. Is that what you're going to tell everyone?

HUGH: No. Just didn't work out. People don't need to know that you were an alcoholic.

MINDY: I think everyone knows that by now.

HUGH: You had to do this in public, of course, while everyone watched. So many of our friends came up to me in private and said, "You better take care of your wife." As if *I* was pumping bottles of rum and Coke down your throat. I was always the designated driver.

MINDY: I haven't had a drop in nine months.

HUGH: I want to see how long that lasts.

MINDY: You're not being very supportive.

HUGH: Duh. Why don't you go outside and wait for the movers?

MINDY: Not right now. I need a break. *(Beat.)* I have one last favor to ask of you.

HUGH: What's that?

MINDY: I'm afraid that I'll never sleep with anyone again once I leave this house.

HUGH: You want to have sex with me? No thanks.

MINDY: No, no, no. Not that. Just cuddling and holding each other.

HUGH: I don't want to see your face ever again. I don't plan to visit you in San Francisco.

MINDY: It's a good opportunity. A fresh start. A new life with new friends.

HUGH: Good for you! I'm happy for you.

MINDY: One more night? Please.

HUGH: No. I don't want any more accidental exposures.

MINDY: Nothing we ever do is an accident. I believe accidents happen for a reason.

HUGH: I didn't know you've become a pop psychologist.

MINDY: I've been studying and trying to rethink my life.

HUGH: Great. Keep rethinking and move.

MINDY: Hugh. Why are you so . . .

HUGH: Have you ever thought about what it feels like to be *me?* You've made me a pea-brained fool in front of everyone. I tried so hard to be nice and understanding, and . . .

MINDY: Maybe sex isn't what it's all cracked up to be.

HUGH: What? How dare you say that? If it wasn't for sex, I wouldn't be stuck with your illness circulating all over my body!

MINDY: You're not sick. You're healthy. You're fine.

HUGH: I'm not fine if I have to orchestrate a schedule of pill-popping every day for the rest of my life. I can't vary my eating schedule because my stomach could have severe side effects if I don't have anything in there. I'm taking *toxic* drugs that can permanently damage my own liver and kidneys. I might as well drink Drano.

MINDY: Then stop.

HUGH: Stop what?

MINDY: Those pills.

HUGH: No.

MINDY: I'm serious.

HUGH: You're insane.

MINDY: You were fine before. You don't have to take everything the doctor tells you to. Do a little research.

HUGH: I should've done my homework on you before I married you in the first place!

MINDY: We did love each other. You still remember that, do you?

[HUGH *nods quietly.*]

MINDY: Please. Let's hang on to that, and forget everything else. It's all smoke and mirrors, but the fire was always there.

HUGH: I'm no longer young.

MINDY: I think if we went out in the world and made things happen for ourselves, we'd never have to feel old again.

HUGH: Maybe. I don't have the energy like I used to.

MINDY: That's okay. I'll always love you no matter what happens.

HUGH: Even if I fall for someone else?

MINDY: Yes. I want you to be happy.

HUGH: (*Beat.*) What's come over you?

MINDY: Sadness. What else can I do?

[MINDY gets up.]

HUGH: Right. Nothing.

MINDY: I think I want to eat alone tonight.

HUGH: Okay. You want me to call Dennis for you?

MINDY: *No.*

HUGH: Why not? I thought he was a friend of yours.

MINDY: He won't have anything to do with me. Thinks I'm going to infect his kids.

[HUGH says nothing.]

MINDY: What do you think of that?

HUGH: I didn't know that I was supposed to give an opinion on everything.

MINDY: You're deaf. You're supposed to have opinions on everything!

HUGH: Sometimes it's better to keep quiet and not judge others so quickly. The world has too many opinions as it is. (*Beat.*) But if you really must know, I think Dennis is a nice guy.

MINDY: You like him now?

HUGH: I thought I told you. His new job is at the IT department at the hospital now. Very helpful with computers.

MINDY: Oh.

HUGH: Funny, isn't it? Time can change so much.

[MINDY nods quietly.]

HUGH: He's still married to Bebe.

MINDY: They made up. That's nice.

HUGH: We've talked about you.

MINDY: You did?

HUGH: Remember that day when I almost broke down because all my data on my computer was lost? He was so patient and he was able to save the hard drive. I was so grateful that I had to forgive him. He thought it was strange that I'd "forgive" him, but when I told him why, he said nothing. We talk now and then.

MINDY: Why didn't you tell me so before?

HUGH: I didn't see the need. You and I weren't talking for a while, remember?

MINDY: Why didn't we *really* talk before?

HUGH: Our timing was never right. I think that's what it is.

MINDY: (*Brightening.*) Maybe we could try again?

HUGH: I'd lose the last of my credibility if I went back to you.

MINDY: (*Beat.*) You've changed so much. You're truly one of them now. And I remember how you used to worry whether they'd accept you.

HUGH: I like it here. Things don't always change so rapidly like they do in the hearing world.

MINDY: True, true. Good ol' Houston. A big city with a small-town heart.

[*HUGH smiles. Door lights blink. MINDY turns to the front door, then to HUGH.*]

MINDY: The movers. They've arrived.

HUGH: I'll go upstairs and stay out of the way.

[*MINDY and HUGH look at each other.*]

HUGH: Go answer the door. A new life's waiting for you.

MINDY: (*Remembers herself.*) Right.

[*HUGH walks offstage while MINDY stands paralyzed in the middle of the living room. Finally: She commands herself to move towards the door.*]

Scene 12: 2002

[MINDY, covered with a blanket, is sitting on the sofa and looking out the window. Her eyes seem a little unfocused. HUGH, now a little older, steps onstage with a bouquet of brightly colored flowers and approaches her. He stops when he realizes she can't quite see him.]

MINDY: Is that you, Hugh? Every night, and every day, you appear clearly as my favorite day back in Texas, where my dreams were as big as the skies that seemed to run forever. You stood there and posed for silly pictures with my cheap camera, and I ran through the waves while you took off your shoes and socks, and you had to put them in the right place before you rolled up your pants before running out to meet me. I pulled you down into the waves, and for a minute there you looked so angry that I had to laugh at how soaked you were. That was our second kiss. Do you remember? Because I do. I've had thousands of days gone, but only one has stayed so clear as glass. I can live forever on that one day, and still be happy.

[HUGH approaches MINDY, who suddenly stops; she has limited vision due to CMV.]

MINDY: Who are you?
HUGH: Hugh. Your ex-husband. Remember me?
MINDY: You look familiar. Come closer.

[HUGH pulls up a chair next to the sofa. She reaches out and touches his face softly, tenderly.]

MINDY: Hugh? You finally came. After so many years . . .
HUGH: I never thought I'd move to the Bay Area, but here I am.
MINDY: You've moved here? For me?
HUGH: No. I got a great job offer at Stanford University.
MINDY: Oh. You still married?
HUGH: Yes. My stepson's living with us now. It's worked out great.
MINDY: You know I can't see very well?

HUGH: I noticed.

MINDY: But I'm okay. I can just sit here and . . .

HUGH: You all right?

MINDY: When my vision started going, I went through all the photographs we took on that day on Padre Island and I memorized all of them so I'd have you and that day to remember. You remember that perfect, *perfect* day?

HUGH: Yes, I did. The only good day of our lives together.

MINDY: All that much pain and so many years for one lousy day, eh?

HUGH: It wasn't lousy. I saw love. I saw love bursting out of your body. I saw love as a shimmering aura around your face. I saw love move through the winds with your hands. I saw love give my heart a new beat, a new meaning. More than that, I *felt* love injected into my veins. I felt loved. I felt I could do anything. I felt I could literally change my life for another person and be happy. I changed my life.

[MINDY reaches for HUGH's hand but instead comes across his bouquet.]

MINDY: Flowers! Thank you.

[MINDY touches the bouquet gingerly and sniffs a few.]

MINDY: Where did you get those?

HUGH: I got those yesterday from a flower shop in Padre.

MINDY: You brought these [*flowers*] all the way from there?

HUGH: I drove out there yesterday morning because I knew I wasn't going back there again, not for a long time. Maybe never. I sat on the western shore, and remembered those days when we thought we knew everything even though we didn't know much then. It was my last moment of peace in Texas, but I was happy to leave.

MINDY: You still love me?

HUGH: A love like ours can never die. It comes and goes, but it is like the waves racing back and forth on the shore.

MINDY: Like Padre.

HUGH: Yes. Like Padre.

MINDY: Where we danced in the water with our clothes on. We jumped up and down and floated like driftwood.

HUGH: Amazing that no one was around to gawk.

MINDY: We had the whole world to ourselves, and the blue skies were the perfect place where we could fall asleep and dream in each other's arms.

HUGH: We couldn't stop laughing and dancing.

MINDY: We didn't need music to help us dance.

HUGH: Our kisses drifted like baby clouds evaporating.

MINDY: Then we trudged out of the water and shivered from the wet.

HUGH: Your hair was like a mermaid's—glistening with pearls.

MINDY: Your chest was covered with some seaweed kelp.

HUGH: We didn't realize how dead we had been living until that moment. We came alive!

MINDY: With each kiss we gave each other, we had to grow up and die.

HUGH: Not to die, but to remember.

MINDY: How could we have ruined so much for each other?

HUGH: We should've visited Padre more often.

MINDY: But we didn't.

HUGH: When you die, you'll always be running like a wild horse on Padre, long before the real estate developers came in and destroyed everything.

MINDY: Only if you'll run free and be with me.

HUGH: (*Thoughtfully.*) Padre Island.

MINDY: Yes. Padre Island. (*Beat.*) The place where all the great blue Texas skies begin.

HUGH: The place where we will always remember love, shivering and shimmying through our veins.

MINDY: No more hurricanes to tear us apart.

HUGH: Just a safe harbor for us, and nobody else. (*Beat.*) Remember that day you asked me to cuddle you one more time? I wish I did.

MINDY: (*Smiles.*) There's still a chance. I've never dreamed of anyone else.

HUGH: Love can never get too much forgiveness.

[*HUGH moves from the chair to the sofa, and puts his arms around her.*

*MINDY closes her eyes with a great deal of pleasure; she is finally con-
tent. She snuggles up to HUGH.*

*HUGH sighs, pulling the blanket over to cover himself as well, and
strokes her hair.*

Lights fade to BLACKOUT.]

Doogle

FOR SEAN VIRNIG, BECAUSE HE'D ASKED FOR THIS.

WITH SEAN VIRNIG AS producer, and Dawn Hill and Paula Schnoor as co-directors, the play premiered at the Minnesota State Academy of the Deaf, Faribault, Minnesota on 7 April 2005.

CAST

TANYA WEBB: Sabra Carlin
CLIFF CLUSTER: Jake Lingle
YVETTE POPPENS: Jenna Poehlmann
MARK MELVIN: Lance Gonzalez
MS. BARBETT: Janna Erlandson
CATE: Kayla Gonzalez
LEO: Dustin Gonzalez
SUE: Rachel McBride
DONNY: David Bowen Jr.
MR. WEBB (FATHER): Daniel Durant
MS. QUINCEY: Brianna Jacoboski
MR. ISEL AND VIDEO RELAY SERVICE (VRS): Brittany Ellenbecker

STAGE CREW

Amanda Jacobson
Kelsey Woodward
Tenja Smith
Chad Johnson
Jessica Novak
Jenny Smith
Kirsten Pudas
Phillip Hillenbrand
Ryan Johnson
Kayla Gonzalez

STAGING CONSIDERATIONS

Minimally, the play requires four teenaged girls and four teenaged boys. One boy (LEO) can also play the male adult characters (WEBB, ISEL, etc.), and one girl (CATE) can also play the female adult characters (VRS, QUINCEY, BARBETT, etc.) as needed. If it's possible to cast separate actors for these adult roles, that's also fine.

Nine lightweight classroom desks are needed for quick and fluid set changes. No special costumes are needed except for the two actors performing the adult roles; they could wear a simple tie or skirt as needed to indicate that they are not teenagers. Because miming props is a natural given in ASL, no hand props are needed. Scene 9 has detailed suggestions for a small make-believe TV. The director may want to consider having three main lighting areas across the stage to help vary the pace of the show and convey different locations.

I can't decide how the word "Doogle" should be signed. Initializing the sign "search" with the letter "d" doesn't quite work for me. It is my hope the directors will come up with the right sign. If there's already a sign for "Google," then it may be easiest to adapt it for "Doogle."

Scene 1. Neutral.

[All EIGHT students line up on the front of the stage. As soon as the first person is done signing, the second person says their next line, and so on.]

TANYA: Once upon a time . . .
CLIFT: A few people came up with the idea . . .
YVETTE: Of the Internet . . .
MARK: In the days of Cold War . . .
CATE: When the United States and Russia . . .
LEO: Built up huge arsenals of weapons . . .
SUE: Ready to attack each other.
DONNY: In 1965, the Internet was born.

SUE: If one country was bombed out of existence . . .

[LEO *falls to the floor. CATE suddenly reaches over to touch SUE's hand.*]

CATE: An email could still go through another country . . .
MARK: And arrive in the United States.
YVETTE: One of the people who helped create the Internet . . .
CLIFT: Was deaf. He couldn't sign.
TANYA: His name was Vint Cerf.
CLIFT: (In case you were wondering.)
YVETTE: But if he were a signer, he'd have invented . . .
MARK: Doogle!
CATE: Each deaf signer is a computer . . .

[CATE *notices LEO still on the floor. She turns to SUE.*]

SUE: We need to repair the computer.

[CATE *and SUE pull LEO up to his feet.*]

LEO: Thanks. Just needed to reboot.
SUE: Anyway . . .
DONNY: Doogle!
SUE: Yes, yes, I remember!
LEO: I swear that you women never forget a single thing.
CATE: That's not true. You guys never forget anything either!
MARK: Doogle works like this . . .
YVETTE: No one enters data about our personal lives . . .
CLIFT: Not on Google, anyway.
TANYA: You see, in our own brains and hands . . .
ALL: We remember.
CLIFT: We have eyes. We never miss a thing.
ALL: We remember.
YVETTE: A teacher says something funny.
ALL: We laugh.
MARK: A friend loans me ten dollars and I forget to pay him back.
ALL: We remind.
CATE: A friend sends me a joke through email.

ALL: We forward.

LEO: A hearing stranger on the street gives us funny looks.

ALL: We remember.

SUE: A boy gives me my first kiss.

ALL: We remember.

DONNY: Look at our hands.

[ALL examine their hands and hold them up for the audience's inspection.]

ALL: We remember.

[Lights BLACKOUT.]

Scene 2. In the hallway outside the cafeteria.

[TANYA stands, busy thumb-typing on her pager, with YVETTE and SUE.]

YVETTE: You finish your English homework?

SUE: No, of course not. I have to work on the yearbook later this afternoon, and then I'll finish my homework tonight.

[TANYA looks up from her pager.]

TANYA: Be with you in a minute.

SUE: She's a real pager junkie. Almost worse than drugs.

YVETTE: Oh, no. Drugs are worse.

SUE: I can picture her now at a hundred years old: all stooped over, typing away.

YVETTE: Who knows what technology will be like by the time I'm a hundred years old?

SUE: The world might be "perfect." No deaf people, no blind people, no disabled people. . . .

[TANYA puts away her pager.]

TANYA: Sorry. What were you talking about?

SUE: About you, of course.

TANYA: What were you saying?

SUE: We were analyzing the way you part your hair.

YVETTE: That's not funny.

SUE: She's a big girl. She can handle it. (*To TANYA.*) Pretty soon no one will remember your face, but they'll all know how your hair looks on top. Your old name sign? Tanya. Your new name sign? (*Gestures the part in TANYA's hair.*)

YVETTE: That's so mean!

SUE: Deaf people need to stop looking down and start looking up. See, we all have faces.

[DONNY enters.]

DONNY: Cafeteria not open yet?

[SUE shakes her head no. DONNY peers through the windows of an imaginary door. He pulls out his pager and checks something on it.]

DONNY: Five more minutes. (*To TANYA.*) How you doing?

TANYA: I slept well.

DONNY: I heard that you have a new boyfriend.

TANYA: What?

[DONNY points to TANYA's pager.]

DONNY: That's *your* boyfriend.

TANYA: Very funny.

SUE: It's true. Can you imagine what Tanya would be like *without* her pager?

TANYA: Oh, no, don't you—

YVETTE: Please leave her alone. Her pager's her business.

[DONNY approaches SUE.]

DONNY: Ready to dissect some frogs in Biology today?

SUE: That's so disgusting.

DONNY: Part of life. We live and we die and then what? We get dissected.

SUE: You got that wrong. People will remember us.

DONNY: We need to do more things and get famous for doing them. Or we could get married and have babies.

SUE: What's with you and the idea of us getting married?

TANYA: Yeah! You've talked almost nothing else since fourth grade.

DONNY: Look at her [SUE]. She's beautiful. I can't believe guys don't want her.

SUE: Stop. You're embarrassing me.

DONNY: I'm sorry. I didn't mean to.

SUE: I just wish that everyone didn't have to know about you and . . . me. I feel everyone's watching me all the time.

DONNY: You're ashamed of me?

SUE: No, no. It's just that . . . I don't know how to explain it.

DONNY: No, no. I get it now. You don't love me, and you don't want to marry me when we graduate from high school.

[DONNY storms off.]

TANYA: (To SUE.) Wow. He really loves you.

YVETTE: (To SUE.) You should at least try to make friends with him.

SUE: Enough of you people tapping on my shoulders!

[SUE storms off and passes CLIFT on his way onstage.]

CLIFT: What was that about?

TANYA: Donny and Sue.

CLIFT: They're getting married?

TANYA: No. Of course not.

[TANYA feels her pager vibrate.]

TANYA: Excuse me.

CLIFT: Pah! You finally say "Excuse me" before you check your pager. Finally, some manners!

TANYA: Very funny.

[TANYA whips out her pager and reads an email.]

TANYA: I have to go. Emergency.

[TANYA scurries off. YVETTE shrugs, at a loss for words. CLIFT peers through the window of the cafeteria's door, and then notices something with the door knob.]

CLIFT: Hey! The door's not locked!

[CLIFT opens the door and invites everyone in.]

Scene 3. The videophone room.

[On stage left, TANYA presses a remote control in front of an imaginary TV screen. On center stage sits a female VRS Interpreter. On stage left stands Mr. WEBB, Tanya's father. In this scene, TANYA signs to VRS in ASL; VRS to TANYA, in ASL, but to WEBB, in SEE; WEBB to VRS, SEE. (SEE represents the spoken English.)]

VRS: (*In SEE; to WEBB.*) Hello, this is Video Relay Interpreter Number 387. I'm calling for a deaf client who will be using sign language to communicate with me and I will voice—
WEBB: (*Interrupts.*) I've used VRS before. Is this Tanya?
VRS: (*Almost at the same time as WEBB.*) Is this Tanya?

[Please note that VRS will sign slightly behind the person talking in the rest of this scene.]

TANYA: (*To VRS.*) Yes, Dad, it's me. You sent me an email. Is something wrong?
WEBB: (*To VRS.*) Ah, yes. I need you to come home this weekend.
TANYA: (*To VRS.*) What's wrong? It's such a long trip home. Four hours, and it's still subzero weather.
WEBB: (*Sighs; to VRS.*) All right, all right. Glass died this morning.
TANYA: My dog? Dead?
VRS: (*In SEE, almost at the same time as TANYA.*) My dog? Dead?

[WEBB turns his face away from the audience as VRS and TANYA exit. Then WEBB turns to the audience.]

WEBB: (*In SEE.*) If I could sign fluently in ASL, I'd tell my daughter this much: (*In ASL.*) "A few years after you started going away to school, I found this mutt limping onto the farm one weekend. You ran straight ahead of me, and you didn't hear me telling you to stop. After all, it was a strange dog. You saw that he had a shard from a beer bottle stuck in his hip, but you went ahead and pulled it right out. Boy, did he bleed but he lay down right in front of you like a lamb. Your mother saw the whole thing from the kitchen window and called the vet. An hour later, you named him Glass and he was yours for life. You couldn't wait to come home on weekends and play with Glass. He never let out of his sight, not for one minute. He followed you everywhere, and the only place he wasn't allowed in with you was church. And I have to tell you, Glass was very lonely when you went away to school during the week. Having another dog in the household depressed him even more. He didn't want Sheba's company; he wanted *your* company, and no one else's. Each Friday night Glass sat out on the front porch and waited with his nose for your driver to bring you up here. He just knew when you'd arrive, and within five minutes before your arrival, he'd start barking. I couldn't see or hear anyone down the road, but he was barking and running happily in circles. Sure enough, he was right. The bright headlights swept from around the bend, and there you were, getting out of the car. Glass was totally beside himself when you arrived. It was as if he'd saved up the energy of his week-long loneliness for the weekend happiness of being with you again. Tell me, Tanya, where did our happiness of being together as a family end? Was it because church was never sign-interpreted for you? Was it because it was too hard for us to learn sign language? Was it because you grew up an hour south of Minneapolis and decided that you were going to be a big city girl instead of returning to the farm like all your brothers and sisters who never left this land? Tanya, look at these hands. All they remember is the land—acres and acres of land, no matter how merciless the weather."

Scene 4. In the cafeteria.

[MARK scurries around with an imaginary video camera and zeroes in on YVETTE, who is eating her breakfast with CLIFT.]

YVETTE: Hey!

MARK: Say something.

YVETTE: No.

MARK: Please.

YVETTE: This is for the school's Web site, right?

MARK: Of course.

YVETTE: Fine. I'm very hungry, and the cafeteria is a great place to be when you're very hungry.

MARK: That's not a very imaginative thing to say. We can't use that on the Web site.

YVETTE: I heard that a guy named Mark Melvin wants to ask me out for the spring prom. Is that true?

[MARK stops.]

MARK: Who told you that?

[CLIFT snickers.]

YVETTE: Doogle told me.

MARK: Doogle?

YVETTE: We deaf people have the same mind, and we know each other's secrets. I thought you knew that.

MARK: You can't read my mind.

YVETTE: No, no—Doogle is just a collective mind. We instinctively know when one of us is hurt badly, and when one of us is deliriously happy with good news. We are a big family with one mind.

MARK: That's not true.

YVETTE: How did I know about you, then?

MARK: Someone told you.

YVETTE: No. No one told me. You've been Doogled.

[MARK walks off with his camera. CLIFT waves for YVETTE's attention.]

CLIFT: You're not going out with him to the prom?

YVETTE: None of your business.

CLIFT: But I saw the whole conversation!

YVETTE: He's a nice guy. But I'm afraid that he doesn't have much of a sense of humor.

CLIFT: Try telling him a few naughty things.

YVETTE: I will not! I want to be nice, and I want the world to be nice, so I have to be nice to help make the world nice.

CLIFT: Nice girl, you.

[YVETTE gives CLIFT a dirty look.]

LEO: (Glances at the clock above them.) Time for class now.

[Lights DIM.]

Scene 5. In Ms. QUINCEY's classroom.

[STUDENTS sit at their desks in a half-circle. TANYA seems particularly despondent. DONNY sits far away from everyone else, and tries not to look at SUE.]

QUINCEY: (To DONNY.) Can you move your desk closer here, please?

[DONNY reluctantly moves his desk, but only by six inches.]

QUINCEY: Closer.

[DONNY moves his desk by only two inches.]

QUINCEY: Come on, closer.

DONNY: Why? Where I'm sitting is perfect for me.

QUINCEY: But not for me.

[DONNY rolls his eyes and moves his desk closer.]

QUINCEY: Thank you. (To STUDENTS.) Today we're going to talk about Web sites.

DONNY: Again?

[QUINCEY gives DONNY a dirty look and continues.]

QUINCEY: Most people think that Web sites have to be all about colors, flashy images, and language dressed up. I'm here to tell you that's *not* what people really want. What they want is information, and they want that information fast. They don't want to waste hours looking around for store hours for a store they've never been to. So I want you to write down on a piece of paper the things you want to see on your own Web site.

MARK: Write down on a piece of paper? Can't we type it up on a computer first?

QUINCEY: Excellent point. But there's something . . . tangible about feeling the electricity of your thoughts surging from your brain right down into your fingers where you must decide what to write. Typing's too easy, in my opinion, when it comes to thinking. We need to think carefully and thoughtfully so that people can appreciate the thought and care we've put into our Web sites. (*Glances at the clock.*) Ten minutes.

[Each STUDENT takes out a sheet of imaginary paper and scribbles. Sometimes they eye each other as if looking at each other would give them a boatload of ideas. Suddenly, the lights dim and the STUDENTS freeze.

SUE breaks out of the frieze and walks to the center stage. As she does so, the other STUDENTS swarm around her. Using their hands and arms, they create what SUE visualizes herself on her home page.

SUE stands frozen, thoughtfully, looking demurely off into space. One of the taller STUDENTS fingerspells above her head: "Tanya Webb," and another STUDENT signs, "Superstar!" On one side of her is another STUDENT who gestures the text and its link next to her portrait: "FILMS." STUDENT #1 clicks on the imaginary word, and in doing so, she spins away from the cluster of STUDENTS.]

STUDENT #1: "Hello, I'm Tanya Webb. Thank you for visiting my home page. I hope you'll get to see some of the clips of my work in all of the movies listed below."

[STUDENT #2 imitates an action heroine who swings a fist against an imaginary villain.]

STUDENT #3: That's from the movie *Charlie's Deaf Angels: Full Signing Ahead.*

[STUDENT #4 gestures a deafblind woman shaking a box full of coins and smiling happily.]

STUDENT #5: That's from the movie *No One Knew Laura,* the story of Laura Bridgman, the first deafblind success story in this country, way before Helen Keller.

[STUDENT #2 gestures a very confident MAD MAX-like warrior making a speech before she goes off on a motorcycle.]

STUDENT #2: (*In mostly gestures; this part should NOT be voiced.*) You-people voice no more, but important heart up-there. You-people ready shoot aliens land. Hands no, voice no. Important heart here. Now fight!

STUDENT #3: That's from the movie *Speechless World.* She won her second Oscar for her performance as Athena, who demonstrates to the entire world struck dumb by an evil alien race that losing one's voice needn't be the end of the world.

[STUDENT #1 spins back into the cluster of STUDENTS, and TANYA walks back to her desk.

STUDENTS go back to their chairs. They glance at each other and scribble down some ideas. Suddenly CLIFT freezes as if in a hip-hop pose, complete with a baseball cap, as imagined on his own home page.

The other STUDENTS cluster around him. One of the STUDENTS fingerspell, "Clift Custer" right in front of his chest. Another STUDENT whips out an imaginary measuring tape and measures him from head to toe, and another STUDENT puts on new clothes for him to wear. CLIFT is definitely phat.

CLIFT breaks out of the cluster of STUDENTS. All of a sudden, life is a music video. The other STUDENTS dance to some imaginary music (if *music is going to be used, use instrumental music with a strong bass line). MARK runs around the stage, using his cinematographer's hands to frame certain images of the STUDENTS dancing, and cutting back and forth between the DANCERS and CLIFT signing his rap-like lyrics:]*

CLIFT: (*In a different dialect that's not typically Clift's.*)
    People out there say that I'm deaf,
    But I'm definitely cool and def.
    Forget all that blink
    On all my gold links.
    Just remember who's the deaf man
    Who's had to fight and understand
    What it meant to give lip.
    Being def and deaf is my trip.

[CLIFT tips his imaginary hat a la the hip-hop star Usher, and freezes. The other STUDENTS flee back to their desks. A look of disappointment crosses CLIFT's face as he walks back to his desk.

    QUINCEY strolls around the half-circle, checking to make sure that STUDENTS are working on their lists.

    STUDENTS freeze when DONNY stands up as if full of pride in front of a mirror. He feels along his jaw to make sure that he's indeed completely clean-shaven and readjusts his tuxedo. Then he pauses to talk directly to the audience.]

DONNY: To be honest, I don't even want a Web site. All I want from this life of mine is to graduate from school, marry a nice deaf woman, find a good-paying job as a woodworker, buy a big house, raise a family of four children, pay my taxes, and spend Saturday nights with friends at the deaf club. So what do I put up as a title on my web site? "THIS DEAF MAN WANTS A SIMPLE LIFE AND NOTHING MORE"?

[DONNY returns to his place among the STUDENTS. He steals a glance at SUE, who then turns to YVETTE. STUDENTS freeze as YVETTE jumps up.]

YVETTE: I know! I want to be a poet!

[STUDENTS *gesture the various creatures and plants of the sea as* YVETTE *expresses an ASL poem using only ONE handshape (Open palm) that could be roughly translated as:]*

YVETTE: As the waves bob up and down
  Away from me,
  I look into the distance
  And see trees undulate.
  I dive under and swim.
  In the murkiness
  I swim past sharks darting around.
  Then I notice on my right the kelp
  Dancing together a tango.
  I swim until I walk out of the sea.
  The island trees there before me:
  I pray as to these gods.
  Something finally falls and splits
  Apart into two halves, two bowls
  Of the milk I drink to breathe.

[YVETTE *bows as in response to applause.]*

STUDENT #1: (*Reads* YVETTE's *bio very drily.*) "Yvette Popens has had 200 books of her poetry published and translated into over 110 languages all over the world. So far she has sold more copies than all of J. K. Rowling's *Harry Potter* books combined. She is proud of the fact that she hasn't sold out to Hollywood, and that she lives quite happily with her husband Mark Melvin and their children in St. Louis Park, Minnesota."

STUDENT #2: Yeah, right. It isn't fair how some people have more money than us.

STUDENT #3: I think her work's great. Poets and teachers should make more money than sport heroes.

STUDENT #2: No one really cares about poetry. It's so boring!

STUDENT #3: A lot of us are poets at heart. Otherwise, why did our inner Harry Potters buy all her books?

[STUDENTS return to their desks, save for YVETTE.]

YVETTE: Each one of us is a dreamer, and our stillborn dreams are poems gone unrecorded.

[YVETTE returns to her desk. QUINCEY claps her hands.]

QUINCEY: Ready to do your Web sites? Let's go to the computer room now.

[STUDENTS exit except for DONNY and SUE.]

DONNY: You okay?

SUE: Yeah, I guess.

DONNY: I'm sorry if I embarrassed you earlier this morning.

SUE: I just hate the fact that our deaf world feels so small.

DONNY: That's why we have Doogle. We are walking scrapbooks of each other's lives. That's why I love this school so much. I know your life story even if I can't say I know you very well. (*Beat.*) All I know is that you're very beautiful, and that I . . . well, you know.

SUE: My parents say that I should go to college.

DONNY: I'll wait for you.

SUE: What if I change?

DONNY: That's okay.

SUE: What if I get really educated, and you start to feel stupid?

DONNY: Better that you be smarter than stupid like me.

SUE: You're not stupid.

DONNY: I can't help it. I'm a simple guy. I know my limitations. I don't have a lot of big dreams. Just you.

SUE: (*Sighs.*) I don't know what to think.

DONNY: Marry me. You can always divorce me later if I don't make you happy.

SUE: You're joking, right?

[QUINCEY returns.]

QUINCEY: We're waiting for you over there.

SUE: Oh, sorry!

[SUE and DONNY hurry after QUINCEY offstage.]

Scene 6. In the hallways.

[MARK aims his imaginary video camera at SUE, who is opening up her locker.]

MARK: Show me what you've got in there.

SUE: No. My stuff's private.

MARK: Please.

SUE: Why do you have to go all over campus with that camera?

MARK: It's my job.

SUE: What if you didn't have a camera?

MARK: I'll think of something. Anyway, show me your locker.

SUE: I don't want the whole world to know.

MARK: The whole world's not always interested in us deaf people. Sad, but true.

SUE: Still, I want some privacy! Move away.

MARK: Please . . . ?

[MARK feels his pager vibrate. He deftly pulls it out of its sheath and whips it open one-handedly.]

MARK: Gotta go.

SUE: Wow. Must've been really something important.

MARK: My girlfriend.

SUE: You have a girlfriend?!?

MARK: Please don't tell anyone.

SUE: Too late now.

[SUE closes her locker shut and exits. Lights CHANGE.]

Scene 7. Neutral/Isel's office.

[MARK sets down his imaginary camera and addresses the audience.]

MARK: I can't believe it. After eight months of instant-messaging and emailing each other, my girlfriend finally got a videophone, and she wants us to talk tonight. Tonight! (*Stops.*) Why am I telling you this? I don't want to get Doogled. Forget that I ever told you any of this, okay?

[*Mr. ISEL, the school counselor, taps him on the shoulder and beckons him to sit down in his office.*]

MARK: What? Oh.

[*MARK sits down.*]

ISEL: How are you doing?
MARK: Good. No complaints so far. I don't need a counselor, so why are you here?
ISEL: Glad you asked. It seems that your mother's really worried about you.
MARK: I'm doing fine. Okay?
ISEL: Do you have friends here?

[*MARK gives a look of shock.*]

MARK: Of course, I do. Whatever made you ask that question?
ISEL: Your mother said that she never sees you with anyone from the neighborhood when you visit home.
MARK: (*Scoffs.*) There's nobody in my neighborhood, period!
ISEL: I realize that your neighborhood's hearing and no one signs, but that shouldn't stop you from making friends.
MARK: You're not my father.
ISEL: Right. But your mother's asked me to help you.
MARK: I don't need help. I'm doing fine, thank you very much.
ISEL: Do you want a girlfriend?
MARK: I already have a girlfriend. (*Stops.*) Sorry, I didn't mean to—
ISEL: If you don't want me to tell your mother, that's your choice. But I think you owe it to her and explain what's going on with you so she won't have to worry so much. You should be glad that she worries about you. It means she loves you.

MARK: She won't like it at all.

ISEL: Why?

MARK: Because I've never met my girlfriend!

ISEL: How did you meet her?

MARK: (*Quietly.*) Online.

ISEL: Ah. Online.

MARK: What's wrong with that?

ISEL: Did she send you a picture of herself?

MARK: Not yet.

ISEL: So she's got to be the most perfect girlfriend you can ever ask for.

MARK: You're making fun of my feelings!

ISEL: Am I?

MARK: I don't like you.

ISEL: Let's talk about that, then. Why don't you like me?

MARK: You're hearing.

ISEL: But I sign. We're not supposed to discriminate against people who sign or don't sign. So why don't you do the same?

MARK: I'm deaf.

ISEL: Ah, deaf. I'm afraid that's not enough in this world.

MARK: Hearing people have ruined this world from day one!

ISEL: I couldn't agree with you more. Now, tell me about this new girlfriend of yours. Does she sign?

MARK: She's deaf.

ISEL: But a lot of deaf people don't sign.

MARK: She's deaf!

ISEL: Okay, okay. What are you going to tell your mother?

MARK: Nothing.

ISEL: She was actually worried that you might be gay.

MARK: My own mother thinks I'm gay?!? I can't believe this!

ISEL: Many gay teens are afraid of making friends because they might get hurt if people find out.

MARK: Well, I'm not gay. I like girls.

ISEL: That's fine. You just need to talk to your mother. That's all.

[MARK nods and leaves ISEL alone on the stage. Lights DIM.]

Scene 8. Outside in the parking lot.

[YVETTE and TANYA stand outside; they're both bundled up and stamping their feet.

On stage right, QUINCEY and SUE sit in a pair of chairs, miming the actions of student driver and driver's ed instructor in DIM lights.]

YVETTE: Sue's a good driver. I can't even parallel-park!

TANYA: This driver's ed class is stupid. Why do we have to take it? I learned how to drive a long time ago.

YVETTE: Not everyone's a good driver.

TANYA: I don't care.

YVETTE: If you don't care, then why am I standing outside in the cold with you?

TANYA: You don't have any friends.

YVETTE: So you're not a friend of mine?

TANYA: I didn't mean it that way. People don't cluster around you.

YVETTE: I'm sorry if I'm not a movie star like you.

TANYA: How did you know?

YVETTE: I thought everyone knew. That you want to be a bigger movie star than Marlee Matlin and Emmanuelle Laborit.

[TANYA says nothing.]

YVETTE: Did I say something wrong?

TANYA: I can't believe you knew that. Who told you?

YVETTE: Nobody. I can read your dreams.

TANYA: Oh, so you're a psychic now?

YVETTE: Not like that. You know Doogle?

TANYA: Yeah?

YVETTE: I Doogle you every time we talk. I add up all the little throwaway comments, the way you watch these movies and TV shows, and the way you study your lines for the spring play. Who doesn't want to be a movie star?

TANYA: But how did you know about Marlee Matlin and Emmanuelle Laborit?

YVETTE: Guesswork. Or as they say around here, you've been Doogled. Friend A may tell me how much you want to be better than Marlee Matlin, and Friend B may tell me how you watched those Emanuelle Laborit's French films, so . . .

TANYA: I hate it when secrets are so obvious.

YVETTE: Maybe that's what you really want.

TANYA: Excuse me?

YVETTE: You want to be famous, but you know it's a real battle to get anywhere in Hollywood, so you go for the next best thing: Doogle. You join in that collective mind, and sooner or later, everyone in the deaf community will think of you as one of their favorite stars even if you've never made a film.

TANYA: I will be a star. And I will make many, *many* films.

YVETTE: Don't you even understand?

TANYA: What? What are you talking about?

YVETTE: You don't need to say, "I *will* be a star." With Doogle, you are already a star. We know your dreams, because your dreams are ours. We may not always know your name, but trust me, we *know.*

TANYA: Just because you come from a deaf family doesn't mean—

YVETTE: My parents explained all this to me. They said that because I was their child, every one of their friends and *their* friends would know who I was before they ever met me. I'm famous already, and I haven't done a thing yet! I'm famous because of my parents, and look at you. You have a grand chance of making it big without people knowing your hearing parents.

TANYA: Well. . . .

CATE: Most deaf people with hearing parents don't always talk about their families. You know why? Because it's so hard to feel a bond in the chasm between two different languages. It hurts.

TANYA: (*Guardedly.*) I manage all right with my parents.

YVETTE: Don't lie to me. (*Beat.*) Your dog died this morning.

TANYA: That's not true! Take that lie back!

[*YVETTE holds her ground steadfastly.*]

TANYA: (*Quietly.*) Who told you?

YVETTE: Nobody. I remember how you used to be when you came back to the school on Sunday nights, and had to tell us all about your dog Glass. I miss those nights because you were so animated. You loved that dog! What happened?

[TANYA stares at YVETTE and then exits.]

Scene 9. In the gymnasium.

[STUDENTS come onstage, panting as if they've just had a workout, and sit down with towels. LEO stands and paces his own breathing.]

SUE: Five minutes' break? We need more time than that.

LEO: How about (*Checks a big clock above them.*) twenty-five minutes?

SUE: (*Sarcastically.*) You're so funny.

CATE: Look over there.

[TANYA is checking her pager.]

DONNY: (*Glances back there.*) You think the teacher will catch her?

SUE: It'll be so interesting to see if anyone could pry that thing from her hands.

[MARK stands up as if ready to alert the teacher.]

YVETTE: Leave her alone.

MARK: Why? No one's supposed to be checking their pagers in class. Campus rules, right?

[YVETTE says nothing. MARK begins to wave his arms when YVETTE stops him.]

MARK: What?

YVETTE: Don't.

SUE: Yvette's a poet.

MARK: So?

SUE: That means she's a romantic. (*Indicates TANYA.*) Maybe she's emailing her boyfriend.

MARK: (*To YVETTE.*) Does she have a boyfriend?

[YVETTE says nothing.]

MARK: Thought so. (*Waves his arms energetically and points to TANYA thumb-typing.*)

SUE: I can't believe you.

MARK: What?

SUE: No one will trust you ever again.

MARK: Sure, people will.

SUE: Not if you've been Doogled.

MARK: No one cares about such little things.

SUE: Oh, yes, people do. So many people have small minds, and only small things can fit inside their heads.

[SUE waves for TANYA's attention. TANYA looks up, notices Ms. BARBETT approaching, and hides the pager.]

BARBETT: (*To TANYA.*) Were you checking your pager?

[TANYA says nothing.]

BARBETT: When I said, "rest," I meant *rest*. No pagers, no worrying about the world outside. Rest means focusing on your own breathing so you can regain your energy for the next workout. It's good to work out, but it's also good to rest. You need both for a good and healthy life.

[BARBETT extends her hand to TANYA.]

TANYA: What?

BARBETT: You know what I want.

TANYA: It's mine, not yours.

BARBETT: You know the campus rules.

TANYA: You can't! It's mine!

[BARBETT doesn't say anything. Her hand is waiting.]

TANYA: This [*the pager*] is my life!

BARBETT: Hand it over now!

[*TANYA shakes her head no.*]

BARBETT: Your family and friends *in flesh* should be your life. Not some names on a tiny screen.

TANYA: You're deaf. You know why pagers are so important—

BARBETT: We deaf people had a life before pagers. (*Tries not to lose her cool.*) Hand it over now, or I'll make everyone stay after school for a thirty-minute workout!

SUE: (*To TANYA.*) Just give it up, okay [*finish*]?

TANYA: You can't do that—!

[*STUDENTS glare at her. TANYA grudgingly hands her pager to BARBETT.*]

BARBETT: Thank you very much. You'll be staying in detention hall right after school today. (*To the other STUDENTS.*) We're going to do some more calisthenics against the wall. (*Points where.*) Come on, everybody!

[*As STUDENTS flock after BARBETT, CLIFT lingers behind.*]

CLIFT: You know what your new name sign is now? (*Demonstrates the new name sign, which is based on using a pager.*) That name sign will follow you for the rest of your life.

TANYA: Very funny!

[*CLIFT scampers off. TANYA rolls her eyes, inhales, and runs after CLIFT.*]

Scene 10. In MARK's dorm room.

[*MARK enters, locks the door, and sits before the TV right in front of the audience. (The TV could be a small rectangular mirror hanging like a plasma TV with its nonreflexive back to the audience.) He turns on the remote control for the TV, pulls out a small piece of paper, and punches in a videophone number. He looks at himself on the TV and touches up on his face, and then smiles as he presses the remote.*]

Suddenly, CATE, a homely girl, appears right behind MARK's shoulder.
(MARK can see her via the mirror and therefore they can see each other.)
CATE smiles with a hint of hesitation.
MARK is clearly put off by what he sees.]

MARK: Hello?

CATE: (*Mouths.*) Hi.

MARK: You deaf?

CATE: (*Mouths.*) What?

MARK: Sorry. (*Gestures.*) Wrong number.

[CATE looks very hurt as MARK presses his remote. As he does so, the lights flicker once. They both speak to the audience. CATE signs in ASL from this point on.]

MARK: She's not my type.

CATE: I thought all you wanted was a smart and intelligent deaf woman.

MARK: I didn't like the way she dressed.

CATE: I thought all deaf people were the same. You, of all people, should be understanding.

MARK: She can't sign!

CATE: I can always learn.

MARK: My friends wouldn't have liked her anyway.

CATE: Are you that cowardly? That you think first of how your friends think of me, instead of how your heart feels?

MARK: I'd have to slow down my signing for her.

CATE: Nothing wrong with that. Hearing people slow down their speaking for me. No difference.

MARK: Everyone would give me funny looks if I went out with an oralist.

CATE: The world's not the same it used to be ten years ago. The world's no longer black and white. It's all gray now.

MARK: And what if she has a cochlear implant?

CATE: Why should anyone judge me if I wanted to hear just a little better? Why should anyone judge me if I wanted to sign a little better? Hmm?

[MARK doesn't answer.]

CATE: Why won't you answer?

[MARK gets up, turns, unlocks the door, and exits. CATE walks around the chair and glances around.]

CATE: Hmm. Your world feels very different from mine. You don't have problems communicating with anyone on campus, and if they don't really know signs, they know how to communicate with deaf people. You don't need to educate anyone on campus about deafness. Wow. Why can't the world be like that? (*Sadly to herself.*) Many times I've wished that I were hearing, but each time I start wishing for what I cannot have, I remember how my older sister Stella felt after she had her first nose job. Growing up, she had a cute button nose, but she wanted to make the ridge of her nose a bit straighter. A few months later she came home to visit and I thought she looked different. Not better or worse; still the same Stella but different. She kept complaining that her new nose was all wrong. (*Beat.*) I know that no matter how much I want to fix my ears or any part of myself to become a better looking person, I will always have issues with one thing or another. I mean, hearing kids at school make fun of me, or they avoid me altogether because (a) I wear hearing aids, (b) I use oral interpreters in some of my mainstreamed classes, which means I can't sit in the back with the cool kids, (c) my speech isn't always easy to understand, and (d) I'm not cheerleader material. My mother says that the world will belong to those who work hard and wait, so I have to be patient while I stand in the hallways by the lockers, waiting for a few geeky friends—my classmates call them "losers," a word I can lipread anywhere—to come up to me for a little conversation. (*Beat.*) That's why I was so thrilled when this guy named Mark Melvin started chatting with me online. He sounded so nice, so smart, and so understanding. Until I met him, I didn't know what kind of man I wanted, but after chatting with him, I knew I had to have a deaf husband. I mean, would I have to explain my communication needs to him? No. He'd totally understand. Not like some of those hearing boys who snickered at me sometimes in class when I had to ask the teacher to repeat so that I could lipread my oral interpreter just to make sure that I understood her question correctly. (*Beat.*) But I didn't expect Mark to be like those hearing boys; I thought he wanted a deaf woman too!

Scene 11. In the yearbook office.

[SUE pulls out a bunch of papers from an imaginary printer. CLIFT walks over. YVETTE is sitting at a desk, checking off items on a list while checking a folio of pictures.]

CLIFT: Printed out all the pictures already?
SUE: Yeah. The new printer's fast.
CLIFT: Lemme see.

[SUE holds up Picture #1.]

SUE: Not bad.

[CLIFT nods in agreement. SUE holds up Picture #2.]

SUE: I like that. What do you think?
CLIFT: If you crop that part out, it could be a nice cover page for the sports section.
SUE: You know, I keep thinking about that idea of yours: Each section cover page should have a great photograph, full-bleed, with *no* words on that page, but the next page would be in full black with the section title in white.
CLIFT: Too radical?
SUE: Oh, no. I've decided to do that. I'll have to ask Mr. Isel first.
CLIFT: I hate it when we have to go to our yearbook advisor. It seems like they don't trust us to do our job.
SUE: I know, but that's the way it goes. The more we work with him, the more we can get what we want to see in our yearbook.

[CLIFT sighs. SUE holds up Picture #3 and gasps. CLIFT guffaws. YVETTE looks up.]

YVETTE: What's so funny?

CLIFT: Mark snapped a picture of Tanya's head while she's bent over with her pager. Spot-on!

[YVETTE stands up and walks over. She smiles in spite of herself.]

SUE: Isn't that cute? Maybe we can use it for the Student Life cover picture.

YVETTE: But that's a bit mean.

SUE: It's true. How many people do you know who do *not* have a pager?

YVETTE: That's not the point. Do our pagers have a life? Or do we have a life? *Student* Life, hello?

SUE: Don't be such a party pooper. I'm the editor-in-chief. Our yearbook needs more humor. Everyone knows Tanya's a pager junkie.

YVETTE: Mr. Isel won't approve the use of that.

CLIFT: We can put it somewhere else. Like in the funny pictures section at the end of the yearbook right before the index.

SUE: Let's see what Mr. Isel has to say.

[SUE sets Picture #3 aside and holds up Picture #4. She lingers a little too long on it.]

CLIFT: That's a good one of your boyfriend. A football star with thighs of lard!

[SUE nearly slams down Picture #4.]

SUE: Donny's not my boyfriend. We haven't even dated!

CLIFT: He wants you big time. Everyone knows that. Just the same as Tanya's pager addiction.

SUE: Shut up, okay?

YVETTE: It's not a bad picture. Donny looks good in that uniform. That could go into the Sports section where we have different outtakes of the uniform shots.

SUE: It's not going into the yearbook at all.

CLIFT: What? Then why did you print it out for?

YVETTE: (*Aside to CLIFT.*) Cut it. (*To SUE.*) If I were the EIC, I'd want to include it. Besides I don't recall seeing any pictures of Donny anywhere in the yearbook besides his school picture. Donny's a good person, and—

SUE: Enough already!

[SUE storms offstage. YVETTE and CLIFT look at each other.]

YVETTE: Why did you have to pick on her?

CLIFT: She's a good friend. She should just chill.

YVETTE: If you have a lot of feelings for someone, it's very easy to feel a lot of hurt if someone makes a little fun of your feelings.

CLIFT: But she's a tough girl.

YVETTE: No one's tough when it comes to love.

CLIFT: How would you know if you've never had a boyfriend?

YVETTE: I just know.

CLIFT: You in love with someone?

YVETTE: Why should I tell you if you just made fun of Sue?

CLIFT: We're good friends, right?

YVETTE: Good friends don't make fun of each other. (*Beat.*) I need to finish my work with that list of seniors who've sent in their stuff.

CLIFT: For the "Words of Advice from the Soon-to-Be-Wise" page?

YVETTE: Yup. (*Sits down at her desk.*)

CLIFT: Anyone missing?

YVETTE: (*Smiles.*) You.

CLIFT: (*Slightly flustered.*) I'll go write something now and email it to you.

[CLIFT exits.]

Scene 12. In the detention hall.

[TANYA sits crouched at her desk in a half-circle of empty desks. She tries to focus on her homework, but she just can't.

QUINCEY sits at the other end of the stage, proofing a student's homework with an occasional glance at TANYA, who gives small smiles. In her hand is her pager, and she glances at it occasionally when she's not writ-ing in her notebook.

MARK appears center stage just out of the line of eye contact between QUINCEY and TANYA, and unnoticed by either. MARK begins thumb-typing on his pager.]

MARK: Hey Tanya. How's life in detention hall?

[TANYA reads the email on her pager and rolls her eyes in response. TANYA eyes QUINCEY and thumb-types quickly.]

MARK: (*Reads simultaneously as TANYA's thumb-typing.*) Okay. Try-ing to do my geometry.

[TANYA gives QUINCEY a tight smile.]

QUINCEY: Something the matter?
TANYA: No. Just trying to figure out my homework.
QUINCEY: Maybe I can be of some help.
TANYA: No thank you.
QUINCEY: Okay. Just so that you know we're here to help you learn.

[TANYA nods and glances sideways at her pager. She reads.]

MARK: Must be tough. Say, I have a tough problem. Maybe you can help me solve it.

[TANYA thumb-types quickly.]

MARK: (*Simultaneously as TANYA's thumb-typing.*) What problem?

[MARK doesn't notice CATE coming onstage next to him; CATE signs in ASL. TANYA continues working on her homework.]

MARK: (*To himself.*) How do I explain?
CATE: Explain that you just saw an ugly girl and that you want to ask a beautiful girl out to the prom.
MARK: (*To himself.*) The prom's only five weeks away.
CATE: This is your senior year, your last year here at this school.
MARK: (*To himself.*) I don't know if Gallaudet will be like this.

CATE: Colleges don't do proms. (*Beat.*) Proms are for kids.

[*MARK turns with a flare to CATE.*]

MARK: I'm not a kid!

CATE: Then grow up and accept that not everyone you love is perfect.

MARK: I don't love you.

CATE: Then why did you sign off on all those emails to me with "ILY"?

MARK: Just an expression. I don't know.

CATE: Words are very powerful things. Be careful what you do with them.

MARK: You know what people say about the Internet. It's so easy to lie online.

CATE: But I didn't. (*Beat.*) I didn't!

MARK: Go away. (*Thumb-types to TANYA.*) Would you like to go out to the prom with me?

[*TANYA reads her pager with her eyes opening. QUINCEY catches this.*]

QUINCEY: What's up?

TANYA: Oh. Just looking at the time [*watch*].

[*QUINCEY points up to the clock.*]

QUINCEY: If you can look up once in a while, you can see it's very easy to see the time. Please bring me your pager.

TANYA: I wasn't using it.

QUINCEY: Please don't argue with me. You're in detention hall because you were looking at your pager when you weren't supposed to. And now you're looking at your pager when you were supposed to be doing your homework?

[*TANYA hesitates. MARK thumb-types.*]

MARK: You still there?

[*TANYA sneaks a quick glance at her pager and shuts it off.*]

MARK: (*To himself.*) Hey! She shut me out!

[*CATE breaks into a cackle and exits. TANYA walks slowly and hands over her pager.*]

QUINCEY: Thank you. (*Beat.*) Looks like I'll have to suspend your pager privileges for a month.
TANYA: A month?!? I can't live without my pager.
QUINCEY: Please sit down and do your homework.
TANYA: This is so not fair!
QUINCEY: Do you want to report to detention hall for a whole week?

[*TANYA says nothing as she returns to her desk.*]

Scene 13. In the cafeteria.

[*CLIFT brings his dinner tray to the table where DONNY and YVETTE are eating.*]

CLIFT: Hello everyone. (*To DONNY.*) Wrestling practice good?
DONNY: Yeah. Good workout. I feel ready to beat the Iowa boys.
YVETTE: I know you will.
DONNY: Thanks.
CLIFT: I saw a picture of you today.
DONNY: Where?
CLIFT: In the yearbook office.
DONNY: What did Sue think?

[*YVETTE looks warningly at CLIFT.*]

CLIFT: What?
DONNY: What are you two talking about?
CLIFT: Sue stared at your picture for a few seconds too long.

[*YVETTE slaps the back of her hand against CLIFT's arm.*]

CLIFT: Hey!
YVETTE: Sorry. (*To DONNY.*) It just happened. Oops.

[SUE enters with her dinner tray and joins the table.]

SUE: (Over-cheerily.) Hello, everybody!

[DONNY looks quietly at SUE, who then turns to YVETTE.]

SUE: You know what just happened?

[EVERYONE at the table leans forward.]

SUE: Tanya's pager privileges have been suspended for a month. A whole month! Imagine that.

CLIFT: Why?

SUE: I'm not sure.

YVETTE: Then how did you know?

SUE: Doogle. I didn't see her, but I felt this strange sense of being disconnected whenever I thought about Tanya.

CLIFT: That's so silly. No one can read people's minds.

SUE: It's not about reading people's minds. All of us deaf people are part of a large animal that moves as one, that feels as one. Someone hurts someone's feelings in Tampa, Florida, and sooner or later, you feel that pain even though you don't know that deaf person in Tampa. That's Doogle at work.

CLIFT: That's hogwash!

YVETTE: Oh, really?

CLIFT: What did you mean by that?

YVETTE: Mark is your best friend. Why?

CLIFT: We just clicked when we met back in first grade.

YVETTE: You two like gadgets. You love your iPod, and he loves his toys. But he doesn't care for music, and you don't care for Web site design or video cameras.

CLIFT: So?

SUE: I remember my mother telling me that when you first arrived, you were really into loud and colorful clothes. She told me that Mark, who you hadn't met yet, would become your best friend because he was always taking things apart and making all sorts of things work. You were already part of Doogle by the end of your first day here!

[CLIFT looks at SUE, then at YVETTE.]

YVETTE: Don't look at me. My mother swears by Doogle. That's how she met my father. My mother had dated this deaf guy for six months, but it didn't work out. A few of her deaf married friends saw how unhappy she was, so they told her to go to this dance hosted by the Nebraska Association of the Deaf in Omaha. They somehow knew that the love of her life would be waiting for her, and the funny thing was, he felt it too. No one had a name for it back then. How do you explain something like that? The word "intuition" doesn't cover it all. That's why when the Internet came along, we suddenly could coin a word to describe this seventh sense that only deaf people have: Doogle.

CLIFT: I wonder if I will ever meet my future wife.

SUE: Just Doogle a little bit, and she'll come to you soon enough.

CLIFT: There isn't a girl here that I like enough to date.

YVETTE: Why are you in such a big rush? I thought you wanted to become a hip-hop star like Usher.

CLIFT: Usher? How did you know?

[YVETTE and SUE look at each other, and shrug their shoulders.]

DONNY: (*To SUE.*) The yearbook going well?

SUE: (*Tightly.*) Yeah. How was your wrestling practice?

DONNY: Great. Iowa will be sorry that I came into town.

[SUE breaks suddenly into a laugh. YVETTE and CLIFT share a glance but say nothing. TANYA enters with her dinner tray.]

CLIFT: Hey, there! You've finally arrived.

[TANYA sits down and starts eating.]

YVETTE: You all right?

[TANYA continues eating.]

CLIFT: Is it true that your pager privileges were suspended?

[TANYA stares at CLIFT.]

TANYA: Where did you hear that?
CLIFT: Doogle.
TANYA: Figures. (*Resumes eating.*)
DONNY: I just want you to know that you have my sympathy.
TANYA: What? No one died.

[DONNY stands up and sits next to TANYA.]

DONNY: I want you to know that if you need a friend, I'm here
    for you.

[SUE hesitates as she watches DONNY.]

TANYA: Well, thank you.
DONNY: We all need to pull together. That's how we deaf people
    can stay strong no matter what happens.
SUE: That's very . . . touching.
DONNY: Deaf people need more teamwork. That's what I've
    learned from sports.

*[SUE smiles quietly. MARK enters with his dinner tray and sits down. He
gives TANYA a dirty look before he starts eating.]*

YVETTE: You all right?
MARK: You know what? I think I'll go sit over there.
CLIFT: Hey, hey now. What's up, man?
MARK: I don't want to talk about it here with everyone watching.
TANYA: (*Suddenly to MARK.*) The answer is no.
MARK: Oh. (*Beat.*) Thank you.
SUE: (*To TANYA.*) What was that all about?
TANYA: It's not important.
DONNY: I'll take you.
SUE: (*Taken aback.*) What was *that* about?
DONNY: She was looking for someone to take her to the prom.
SUE: I thought Mike Nelson from the Iowa School for the Deaf
    was planning to ask her out.

TANYA: He never did. I know he wants to, though.

DONNY: (*To TANYA.*) I have my own car.

TANYA: (*Quietly.*) Thank you.

SUE: (*Quietly; to DONNY.*) I thought you. . . .

DONNY: You keep saying no. Everyone keeps saying that you're ashamed of me because I'm not as smart like you.

SUE: That's not true.

DONNY: But Doogle doesn't lie. I can feel how a person truly feels about someone, and. . . .

SUE: Oh. I see.

YVETTE: (*Glances at Mark, then to EVERYONE.*) I don't have a prom date right now. But I'm okay with that. My man will arrive and then I will marry him.

MARK: What makes you so sure of that?

YVETTE: My heart and soul is already part of Doogle. It's out there, vibrating and humming along in the veins of the big one animal that we are. Sooner or later, someone who feels my heart and soul will Doogle me, and he will come to me with love radiating from his eyes.

CLIFT: Hey, come on. I think you're pushing it.

YVETTE: I can't help what my heart feels. After all, I'm a poet.

CLIFT: (*Sarcastically.*) Right. I forgot. (*Beat.*) I'm going now and do some homework, and then I'll catch you guys at the TV lounge.

DONNY: Later!

[*CLIFT picks up his dinner tray and exits.*]

DONNY: (*To TANYA.*) We can talk more later about the prom.

[*TANYA responds with a smile.*]

DONNY: (*To EVERYONE.*) Gotta do my homework.

YVETTE: See ya later!

[*DONNY exits. Without any further ado, MARK gets up and leaves without saying another word. YVETTE and SUE exchange glances.*]

TANYA: What?

YVETTE: Mark asked you out?

TANYA: Yeah, but I had to turn off my pager when I handed it over to Ms. Quincey.

SUE: I can't imagine you without a pager now.

[TANYA nods.]

YVETTE: Are you going to be all right?

TANYA: (*Explodes.*) Why do you have to keep asking that of everyone? Why do you have to be so sugary nice?

YVETTE: (*Beat.*) I thought you understood Doogle. I truly thought you did. You hurt one deaf person, you hurt all deaf people. You care for one deaf person, you care for all deaf people. I want to be friends with everyone.

TANYA: Oh, you have plenty of them.

YVETTE: I thought I was obvious. I want *more* friends. More specifically, more deaf friends. The Internet has brought more deaf friends from all over the world that much closer to home.

SUE: Oh, great! Next thing I know, you'll become the United States ambassador for the U.D.N.

TANYA: U.D.N.?

SUE: United Doogle Nations.

YVETTE: Very funny.

SUE: Why not? You can travel all over the world and learn different sign languages. Maybe you can become a bilingual translator—translate poems performed in French Sign Language into English for publication!

YVETTE: (*Quietly.*) That's an awesome idea.

TANYA: Who knows, you might be able to write a love poem to Mark.

YVETTE: Why. . . .

SUE: Looks like you've been Doogled.

YVETTE: (*Slightly irritated.*) Of course.

SUE: It's so hard to keep secrets when you're part of Doogle. Dreams leak, and once you've told a person a secret, it's no longer a secret. Just a hidden link waiting to be clicked on inside Doogle.

YVETTE: All I wanted from Mark was to be asked out to the prom!

[SUE reaches over and hugs YVETTE.]

SUE: You still have a chance. He broke up with his girlfriend.

YVETTE: He had a girlfriend? Since when?

SUE: Not really a "girlfriend"—just some girl he met online.

YVETTE: (*Resignedly.*) Oh.

SUE: You okay?

YVETTE: Yeah, I guess. (*Beat.*) Just can't believe I didn't feel that part of him. I always thought he was available.

SUE: Maybe he's confused about himself. Not sure about his feelings, about life in general. Maybe you should go talk with him in private.

TANYA: Sounds like a good idea. We get enough misunderstandings around here. (*Checks the cafeteria clock.*) We gotta go. Cafeteria's closing in five minutes.

[SUE and YVETTE hurry offstage while TANYA stays behind to finish the last of her meal. Lights BLACKOUT.]

Scene 14. Neutral.

[TANYA stands up and addresses the audience.]

TANYA: As I walked out of the cafeteria into the wide open spaces of the campus green, I saw the nakedness of trees holding up the few buds of spring in the twilight against the moon soon to come. I thought of my dog Glass, who'd have been so proud and happy walking right beside me right there if the school allowed him on campus, and how dead I felt inside. My heart was a snow globe that I kept shaking but no snow would swirl. Why did he have to die? (*Beat.*) Out there in the chilly night I saw the world crack open like a dark blue egg, and out came flickers of flame into my eyes. Suddenly I remembered: Up north I used to be so contented running across the fields with Glass chasing my heels, watching the bees hop from flower to flower, and feeling the sun across my back. There in the distance were my parents sitting on the front porch, drinking lemonade and beer while talking with a few neighbors from the farms nearby. They waved to me, and I waved right back. Why couldn't life be that simple? Just waving to each other, and not having to say anything?

[Lights BLACKOUT.]

Scene 15. The computer room.

[DONNY, MARK, and CLIFT are typing away at their own computers, taking down notes while searching for information. Suddenly—THEY stop.]

DONNY: (*To his computer.*) Hey!
CLIFT: (*To himself.*) Oh, man.
MARK: (*To DONNY and CLIFT.*) I bet it's another virus.

[DONNY moves to reboot his computer.]

MARK: Don't restart the computer. Just leave it.

[CLIFT pulls out his pager and thumb-types a message. Meanwhile, DONNY turns to MARK.]

DONNY: If this is a worm virus . . .
MARK: Just let it sit there. Sometimes if you try to quit a program, the virus will start replicating through the network.
DONNY: Why do people have to do that? I need to do my homework.
MARK: Some people have a very warped sense of humor.

[CLIFT looks up from his pager.]

CLIFT: Just emailed the IT guy. Hopefully he'll come by on campus and fix these computers.

DONNY: But how am I going to do my homework? I have to write a biology paper on pheromones.

[MARK stands up and notices something on an imaginary bookshelf in front of the audience.]

MARK: Get a whiff of that!

[CLIFT walks over to MARK.]

DONNY: (Joins MARK.) What?

MARK: Books. Look. Remember when we were kids, we had to look up the encyclopedia for anything we wanted to learn more about? (To DONNY.) I bet you can find the information you need for your biology paper.

[DONNY scans the book spines until he sees the encyclopedia's "P" volume. As he pulls the book off the shelf, MARK and CLIFT sneeze from the dust flying off the book.]

DONNY: Wow. The dust's really thick.

[As DONNY opens the book, MARK and CLIFT fade away. Lights DIM into a spotlight on DONNY.]

DONNY: Pheromones. (As if reading straight from the book.) "A chemical substance, when released by an individual into the environment, that often causes specific reactions in other individuals." (To the audience.) All my life everyone has known that I am different. I look the same as everyone else, but everyone knows that I am different. It's as if my deafness is a bad pheromone floating in the air ahead of me, as if I am a dangerous contagion that could infect others with the nightmare of never hearing again. Or is it my ordinary intelligence that puts some people off? I can't help it if I'm not an Einstein or a Shakespeare or a Michelangelo. Or is it my loneliness for a woman like Sue? I want her. I'll tell you why I want her. She makes me want to become a better person, and it's for her that I'm willing to study some boring textbooks. I know I'm not cut out for college, but

I'm willing to try and make her happy. (*Beat.*) Every time I walk past her, I catch a scent of her that reminds me again how much more wonderful love can be. Yes, I admit it: I love her. I don't even have to say these words to you. You've already Doogled me a long time ago, so I don't need to justify why I love her so. My heart is a huge organ pumping out vast perfumes of love's pheromones into the air whenever she walks in a mist past me.

[*Lights DIM.*]

Scene 16. The TV lounge.

[*MARK enters to find YVETTE sitting alone and watching TV.*]

MARK: You're alone? No one's here?

YVETTE: The housefather went to the bathroom. He'll be right back. Nothing wrong with that, is there?

MARK: No. Just . . .

[*YVETTE glances around and beckons MARK to sit next to him.*]

YVETTE: Why did you ask Tanya out to the prom?

MARK: Just felt like it.

YVETTE: I always thought you were going to ask me.

MARK: Whatever gave you that idea? I mean . . .

YVETTE: I felt it the last few months.

MARK: That's preposterous. I don't think that far ahead. And you were very, very wrong about Doogle.

YVETTE: Maybe that's true. But you know what they say about the heart and the brain? Sometimes they don't communicate with each other, so the heart is way ahead of the brain and the brain doesn't know it until it's too late.

MARK: What are you trying to tell me?

YVETTE: Why are you so afraid to ask me out?

MARK: You'd laugh at me.

YVETTE: Do I seem like someone who'd laugh at you?

MARK: (*Quietly.*) No.

YVETTE: Then ask me out.

MARK: I can't. I promised Tanya.

YVETTE: (*Sighs.*) Well, if for some reason Tanya changes her mind, you know where to find me.

MARK: (*Awkwardly.*) Thanks. (*Beat.*) Guess I should go now.

[MARK leaves. Lights DIM.]

Scene 17. The videophone room.

[*On stage left, TANYA presses a remote control in front of an imaginary TV screen. On center stage sits a female VRS interpreter. On stage left stands Mr. WEBB. In this scene, TANYA will sign in ASL; VRS to TANYA, in ASL, but to WEBB, in SEE; WEBB to VRS, SEE. (SEE represents the spoken English.) In this scene VRS will be slightly behind either TANYA or WEBB whenever she repeats what they say to each other.*]

WEBB: Tanya! What a big surprise.

TANYA: (*A little embarrassed.*) Well, I just needed to talk to you.

WEBB: Tanya, you're *always* welcome to talk with me at any time.

TANYA: Well, I have a problem.

WEBB: Mr. Virnig has already explained the situation, and—

TANYA: I'm not asking for a new pager, Dad.

WEBB: You aren't? What happened?

TANYA: Some kids were making fun of me. (*Beat.*) I guess they were right. I'm a pager junkie.

WEBB: Well, at least you're not into drugs or alcohol or anything of that, aren't you?

TANYA: No, no. I'm clean. I'm fine.

WEBB: (*Relieved.*) Oh, good. You don't know how much we miss you up here.

TANYA: (*Nods.*) I want to go home.

WEBB: The school isn't working out for you?

TANYA: Oh, I love it here. This school's great! Just that I didn't realize how much I missed you and Mom and . . .

WEBB: I know. But you do need your education. That's why we decided that having deaf friends would make you happier. There aren't any deaf people up here in these parts.

TANYA: I know. But sometimes I wish you'd learn to sign.

WEBB: You know what they say? Sometimes you can't teach an old dog new tricks. I'm an old dog.

TANYA: I don't believe that! You're my Dad! If you and Mom can come down once in a while . . .

WEBB: It's a long ways.

TANYA: I'm not worth it?

WEBB: No, no. (*Sighs.*) Maybe I should learn how to use the computer.

TANYA: If you can drive a tractor through the corn fields, you can learn to drive a computer.

WEBB: (*Chuckles.*) You're a tough farmer's daughter, I'll tell ya that.

TANYA: (*Smiles.*) I'll ask Steven and see if his brother is coming down to pick him up, and if so, I'll catch a ride upstate to you this Friday.

WEBB: (*Quietly.*) You're serious?

TANYA: Yes. I just need to see you and Mom *in person*. I don't want you and Mom to die away, neglected and forgotten like my dog Glass.

[*WEBB inhales, fighting the urge to cry.*]

TANYA: Dad? You all right?

WEBB: (*Exhales.*) Yes, I'm fine. Want to talk to Mom?

TANYA: Yes.

[*Lights DIM.*]

Scene 18. Neutral.

[ALL line along the front of the stage. As soon as the first person is done signing, the second person says their next line, and so on.]

DONNY: Once upon a time . . .

YVETTE: We deaf people were wary . . .

LEO: Of hearing aids . . .

SUE: Bulky TTYs . . .

MARK: Computers . . .

TANYA: Then email appeared.

CLIFT: Suddenly we became better typists!

CATE: The problem was . . .

CLIFT: We didn't feel the need to get together . . .

TANYA: Like before, when we had captioned films . . .

MARK: My parents told me stories about those days . . .

SUE: I think the deaf community was stronger . . .

LEO: Every get-together was a family reunion!

YVETTE: Doogle was so strong in those days.

DONNY: We always had the latest version . . .

YVETTE: The best days of our lives . . .

LEO: And the worst days too . . .

SUE: Each time we lost someone . . .

ALL: *(Simultaneously.)* It hurt.

MARK: The memorial services went on for hours.

ALL: *(Simultaneously.)* On and on!

TANYA: But the stories they told . . .

ALL: *(Simultaneously; NOT voiced.)* Whoa.

CLIFT: Now each generation gets archived . . .

CATE: Indexed and cross-referenced . . .

CLIFT: Not all of us have the latest versions . . .

TANYA: My Doogle program is at version 4.1.7.

MARK: 4.2.1.

SUE: 5.3.

[ALL eyes turn to SUE.]

SUE: I can't help it if I have the *latest* version of Doogle. So if you want the latest news on your deaf friends, you come straight to me.

LEO: Each of us is a tech support person . . .

YVETTE: Easy to contact us . . .

DONNY: Pager . . .

YVETTE: Email . . .

LEO: TTY . . .

SUE: Fax . . .

MARK: Videophone . . .

TANYA: Snail mail . . .

CLIFT: Relay interpreter . . .

CATE: Or a heart-to-heart hug.

CLIFT: That's what Doogle should be . . .

TANYA: No bugs . . .

MARK: No viruses . . .

SUE: No spyware . . .

LEO: No Trojan worms . . .

YVETTE: No spam . . .

DONNY: Simple and clear-eyed as love.

[YVETTE suddenly collapses. DONNY reaches out over her and touches LEO.]

LEO: (*Prompted.*) Simple and clear-eyed as love.

[Meanwhile DONNY helps YVETTE to her feet.]

SUE: Simple and clear-eyed as love. (*Suddenly.*) Carbon-copy!

MARK & TANYA: (*Simultaneously.*) Simple and clear-eyed as love!

CLIFT: Blind carbon-copy!

[CATE closes her eyes and reaches out to touch CLIFT's hand.]

CLIFT: (*Into CATE's hand.*) Simple and clear-eyed as love.

CATE: (*Eyes still closed.*) Ah, Doogle. Who needs technology when all I want is a light touch, a tender hug from all my deaf friends?

[*OTHERS converge around CATE into a huge group hug and smile. Lights on them DIM, then BLACKOUT*]

Whispers of a Savage Sort

FOR MATTHEW

WHISPERS OF A SAVAGE SORT received its workshop premiere at the first New American Deaf Play Creators Festival (Kelly Morgan, artistic director) at the National Technical Institute for the Deaf, Rochester, New York, on 11 September 1996. Produced by Mary Vreeland, the play was directed by Howie Seago. The set and lighting design was by Michael Angelo Tortora; the costume design, Damita Peace; the sound design, Peter Reeb; and the stage manager, Robin Whittaker. The cast was as follows:

GUS: Nat Wilson
NAN: Phyllis Frelich
BILL: Patrick Graybill
DARCY: Elena Blue
VICKI: Mel Westlake
RUMORS: Ashanti Brown, Isias Eaton, Matt T. Hochkeppel, Steve Mularski, Kaysy Sabandith

Voice interpretations were performed by Steven Buescher, Jo Ellen Clark, Ricky Feldman, Tracy Gilbert, and Andrea Jordan. (They voiced from offstage; however, the voice actors themselves should play Rumors in all subsequent workshops and productions.)

STAGING CONSIDERATIONS

Dramatis Personae

GUS Horton, hard of hearing and in his forties, is the associate vice president of the local bank; he speaks and signs very well. He began learning ASL at the age of twenty-two when he met Darcy, his wife.

DARCY Horton, raised in the deaf residential school nearby and now in her forties, works as a word processor.

BILL Rozwell, a residential school graduate and president of the deaf bowling league in his forties, works in a graphic production center.

NAN Rozwell, Bill's wife in her forties, has been Darcy's best friend from their early school days; she volunteers most of her time at deaf-related organizations.

VICKI Harp, a beautiful deaf woman in her thirties, works as a librarian at the local residential school.

RUMORS and other stock characters are played by five voice actors/interpreters (three women, and two men); they stay on stage at all times, constantly *watching* others onstage without drawing attention to themselves.

The stage is divided into thirds: On stage right, the Horton household reflects a different—and a little more upscale—aesthetic than the Rozwell household on stage left. The middle area is used for scenes that don't take place in either house.

ACT ONE

[Lights open softly on RUMORS standing in silhouette backstage with their backs to the audience. They ad-lib/gesture/repeat typical responses upon hearing imaginary gossip; they sign very slowly and exaggeratedly so not to distract the audience's attention on each of the five characters soon to be spotlighted. (RUMORS are not voiced in the beginning.)]

RUMOR #1: Really?

RUMOR #2: Imagine.

RUMOR #3: That's so awful.

RUMOR #4: Oh, wow.

RUMOR #5: I can't believe it.

RUMOR #1: You serious?

RUMOR #2: He asked for it.

RUMOR #3: Oh, come on.

RUMOR #4: How did it happen?

RUMOR #5: You're kidding me.

[Meanwhile: The five main characters are placed strategically onstage. Lights open on GUS, who stands processing a check-cashing request. He turns to the audience and counts the tens.]

GUS: (*Mouths to imaginary customer.*) Ten, twenty, thirty, forty. There you go. Thank you and have a nice day.

[Lights off GUS. Lights on NAN, stirring a pot on the stove. She sticks her finger in and tastes. She realizes it needs more seasoning. She opens the cabinet above the stove and looks for the right spice. She sprinkles it liberally into the pot and puts the spice away. She sticks her finger in for another taste: Not bad. Well, good enough.

Lights off NAN. Lights on BILL. He goes through the motions of making sure that the colors on the huge posters just printed out are correct. He finds the third poster wrongly printed, and puts it aside. He checks his watch against at the clock, and sighs. It's going to be a long day.

Lights off BILL. Lights on DARCY. She is at her computer when an imaginary hearing coworker enters her office and deposits some papers on her desk. DARCY gestures/questions her coworker to make sure she understands what she's supposed to do next. She smiles and resumes keyboarding.

Lights off DARCY. Lights on VICKI. She pulls along an imaginary library cart of books and plucks a book out. She opens it and rifles through it. Interesting. She closes the book, and scans the Dewey numbers on the shelves for the book's rightful place. She puts the book away. As VICKI moves around the cart and steps downstage, the RUMORS turn to observe her.]

RUMORS: (*All pointing to VICKI.*) Whoooo?

[VICKI goes up to the imaginary information counter at the bank.]

VICKI: (*Gestures/signs.*) I would like to open a new account, please. (*Pointed stage right to GUS.*) There? Thank you.

[Lights on GUS. He turns to VICKI.]

GUS: (*Signs.*) Hello, may I help you?

[*VICKI reacts as in "You're deaf too?"*

Lights change. BILL hurries on to his wife NAN at home; GUS and DARCY arrive home from work. Both couples go rapidly through the typical after-work routines and last-minute flurries before they all go off to the bowling alley. GUS and DARCY go offstage.

Lights change to the bowling alley. RUMORS turn around as BOWLERS greeting each other and slapping high fives. BILL and NAN arrive, ad-libbing greetings to fellow BOWLERS.]

BILL: Where's Gus and Darcy?
NAN: I'm surprised they haven't arrived yet.
BILL: Yeah. They're usually on time.

[*BILL is about to collect membership dues when GUS, DARCY, and VICKI arrive.*]

NAN: Oh, there they are!
BILL: Hey! How are you two doing?
DARCY: Just great. Good to see you.
GUS: I'm sorry we're so late. We had to pick up a new friend here.
    I just met her this morning at my bank when she was setting
    up her new account.
NAN: (*To VICKI.*) Where do you work?
VICKI: At the deaf school. I'm a "media resources coordinator"—
    a librarian, you know?
NAN: Funny how hearing people have to come up with more
    fancy words all the time.
DARCY: Oh, I'm sorry. I forgot to introduce everyone.
GUS: Excuse me—I gotta collect the rest of our membership dues.
BILL: I'll be with you in a minute.
DARCY: This is Vicki Harp, and this is Bill Rozwell, and his wife,
    Nan.
VICKI: Very pleased to meet you two.

[*VICKI gives BILL a flirtatious smile. NAN holds her tongue.*]

BILL: I'd love to chat with you, but I—
NAN: Why don't you go on and help Gus?
BILL: Unh, yes.

[BILL joins GUS.]

NAN: (To VICKI.) Where are you from?
VICKI: Kansas City.
DARCY: She's been here only a week.
NAN: Do you like your new job? Who do you work for?
VICKI: So far so good. My boss is Ginny Vargas.
NAN: Oh, I know who she is. She's fascinating.

[BOWLER #1 comes up to DARCY.]

BOWLER #1: Can we talk in private?
DARCY: Oh, sure. (To VICKI and NAN.) Excuse me—I'll be right
    back.
NAN: I'll hold a seat for you at our corner. Like always.
DARCY: Thanks.

[DARCY and BOWLER #1 go off. VICKI and NAN are alone, and they
watch BOWLER #2 go through the motions of bowling a perfect strike.
BILL and GUS slap high-fives with BOWLER #2. VICKI turns to NAN.]

VICKI: What do you do for a living?
NAN: I volunteer a lot. I like helping other people.
VICKI: Like what?
NAN: Oh, I get together with other women and make all sorts of
    things to sell and get money to help other deaf organizations
    here.
VICKI: That's so nice. What does your husband do?
NAN: Careful—don't you fall in love with him.
VICKI: What?
NAN: I'm just warning you—there are no single deaf men left in
    this town. Why did you come here?
VICKI: I was offered a job here.
NAN: If you get lonely, what would you do?

VICKI: I'd chat with you. (*Beat.*) I'm not looking for anyone. If the right man shows up, fine. If he doesn't, that's fine too.

NAN: I see. Just stay away from my husband. And from Darcy's husband. Too many high school sweethearts have married already. I'm just warning you—understand?

VICKI: Excuse me. Hope you'll be more cheerful the next time we meet.

NAN: Hah!

[*VICKI goes off and sits next to BOWLER #3, near GUS and BILL. BOWLER #4 goes through the motions of bowling a gutter ball. GUS makes the notation.*]

GUS: (*To BILL.*) I'm going to the restroom.

[*GUS exits as BOWLER #5 approaches NAN.*]

BOWLER #5: How's your daughter Barbara doing?

NAN: Fine.

BOWLER #5: Where's she now?

NAN: Oh, in New York City. Working.

BOWLER #5: I see. Tell her hello for me.

NAN: Will do. Get Darcy for me.

[*BOWLER #5 goes off and nudges DARCY. NAN beckons DARCY over.*]

NAN: Look at her [*Vicki*].

DARCY: So? What's wrong?

NAN: Don't you recognize her name: Vicki Harp?

DARCY: Never heard of her until tonight.

NAN: She sleeps around. Her specialty is married men.

DARCY: Oh, come on. You can't believe everything you hear.

[*VICKI is laughing at some joke BOWLER #3 has just told. GUS returns from the bathroom, and VICKI glances at him sitting down next to her. VICKI turns back to BOWLER #3.*]

NAN: *Married* men.

DARCY: She wouldn't dare start an affair here—too obvious.

NAN: But look at her. Watch.

[Meanwhile GUS searches under his bench and then around his bench.]

GUS: The money's gone!
BILL: What money?
GUS: The bowling money—$800.
BILL: Where did you put it?
GUS: Over here. (*Stops.*) Wait a second. (*Looks around for it.*) Shit. Maybe someone took it while I was in the bathroom.

[BOWLERS gather round.]

BILL: Why didn't you give it to me?
GUS: Damn! (*Looks around some more.*) Where's the money?
BILL: Wait. Let's really look more carefully. Maybe it got moved around by mistake.

[DARCY follows NAN to where BILL and GUS are looking.]

GUS: Now we can't afford a nice awards banquet like last year's.
NAN: What? What happened?
BILL: Seems we have a thief here.
NAN: (*Goes off.*) We should lock all the doors and search every pocket in this place.

[BILL tries to restrain NAN, more so when she tries to poke into everyone's pockets.]

BILL: Hey! Enough!
GUS: The cash was in a green zippered bag.

[EVERYONE searches all over the place.]

GUS: (*More to himself than to OTHERS.*) Damn. I wish—everyone wrote checks or something.
VICKI: Maybe you should ask the manager.
NAN: You're new here, so butt out.
DARCY: She's trying to help.

[NAN gives DARCY a look.]

BILL: You're the league treasurer. What are we going to do?

GUS: I don't know.

DARCY: Why don't we backtrack and see how we might've overlooked it?

VICKI: How long were you in the bathroom?

NAN: Stop butting in.

VICKI: Excuse me!

BILL: (*To NAN.*) We've got to work together and find that money.

GUS: I still can't believe I left that bag over there. How could I have been *so* stupid to—?

DARCY: It's all right. We'll find the money. (*Beat.*) I should've watched the bag for you.

GUS: You were in that corner gossiping away.

DARCY: We don't gossip. We share *news*.

GUS: Whatever. The money's gone.

BILL: Calm down. We'll take care of everything.

GUS: But-but—

BILL: We'll take care of everything. Trust me.

[GUS searches his own bag and kicks his bag downstage.]

BILL: Relax. You should go have a drink. (*To DARCY.*) Take him home.

GUS: I just feel so . . .

DARCY: Come on.

[GUS and DARCY exit. BOWLERS and VICKI turn to NAN and BILL.]

BOWLER #1: I can't believe it.

VICKI: We still haven't looked hard enough.

NAN: You're a real detective.

BILL: Vicki's right. We haven't—

NAN: Other people are leaving. Look.

VICKI: I'll stop them.

BILL: What for? Half of the people have left already.

BOWLER #2: Think Gus took the money?

BILL: Of course not. He doesn't need the money.

BOWLER #3: How do you know? He's gotta show off how cheap your house looks.

NAN: That's not nice. We've known Gus for twenty-four years. You think we'd be friends with a liar?

BOWLER #4: Maybe he's fooling you.

BOWLER #5: Sometimes people lie.

BILL: But not Gus. He's the most honest man I know. It's gotta be someone else.

NAN: Who?

[VICKI gives NAN a suspicious look as lights fade. Lights open on GUS and DARCY in their bedroom.]

GUS: That was so odd—Bill wanting us to go home. Early.

DARCY: You're never this upset. He meant well.

GUS: I don't want anyone to start making up stories about me.

DARCY: No one will.

GUS: You think so? I can replace the money if I have to, but if they start to tell lies about me, I can't replace my own reputation.

DARCY: Relax. Hey, relax.

GUS: I can't!

DARCY: You don't have to be paranoid about gossip all the time.

GUS: I'm a banker. I have a reputation. Okay?

DARCY: Come, come. Everyone knows you're a good man.

GUS: That didn't stop anyone three years ago.

DARCY: I've seen this happen over and over again. It's nothing new.

GUS: Well, I don't like it. Do I have to watch every *little* thing I do? God, it's as if the deaf community's a nest of spies.

DARCY: We're not bad people.

GUS: Oh, why can't the deaf community be more like a family?

[Lights off GUS and DARCY. Lights on BILL and NAN in their own bedroom. They stand as if lying on their backs in bed.]

BILL: I don't know. We've gone over this already. Can't I sleep?

NAN: You got something to hide?

BILL: Everybody hides from you. (*Beat.*) If *I* had secrets, I wouldn't tell you.

NAN: I'm your wife!

BILL: But you don't know how to keep your mouth shut.

NAN: Yes, I do. (*Beat.*) Barbara. No one knows.

BILL: I'm impressed.

NAN: (*A long pause.*) Maybe Barbara'll come back.

BILL: Oh, sure! This ain't Hollywood.

NAN: She just has to say sorry.

BILL: How? (*Moves away.*)

[Lights off BILL and NAN. Lights on GUS and DARCY.]

DARCY: Families do fight. Even the good ones.

GUS: (*Sighs.*) We've had this talk before.

[Lights dim on GUS as lights go on RUMORS. Each RUMOR speaks as a younger GUS, maturing in his relationship with DARCY; each RUMOR speaks to DARCY.]

RUMOR #1: (*With a beginner's signing awkwardness.*) I'm only learning. They should be more—what's the sign for "patient"?—patient.

DARCY: You'll do just fine.

RUMOR #2: (*With less signing awkwardness than RUMOR #1.*) Why does it have to matter so much that I'm hard of hearing? What's the big deal?

DARCY: You'll do just fine.

RUMOR #3: (*With more signing fluency than RUMOR #2.*) I can't believe they don't want to be my friend. I mean, we *all* have problems in the hearing world.

DARCY: You'll do just fine.

RUMOR #4: (*With increased fluency in signing.*) I look at the deaf community, and then I look at you. I'm amazed you even married me. (*Beat.*) Why are they so obsessed with gossip?

DARCY: (*Softly.*) You'll do just fine.

RUMOR #5: (*With GUS's current signing fluency.*) Why do people have to spread rumors? I mean, why? The second we're born, we're all infected with this incurable sickness. It seems like we spend all our lives, either spreading rumors or trying to stop them.

[*Lights off RUMORS. Lights on GUS as DARCY turns to GUS.*]

DARCY: You'll do just fine.

GUS: (*Looks at her; a beat.*) You've said the same thing all these years, and has anything changed? No.

DARCY: Maybe someone will find the money tomorrow. Come to bed.

[*GUS paces again.*]

GUS: I know I won't be able to sleep. (*Beat.*) I'm going out for a walk. (*Kisses DARCY on the forehead.*)

[*GUS exits. Lights off GUS and DARCY. Lights on BILL and NAN.*]

NAN: (*Softly.*) Look at me. Please. I tried my best. You don't want me around your friends, I stay home.

BILL: Oh, never mind. (*Turns over to sleep.*)

[*NAN touches BILL gently on the shoulder.*]

NAN: I've been thinking.

BILL: I don't wanna stay up all night.

NAN: I want to make it up to you.

BILL: For starters, stop talking about people.

NAN: You like gossip too.

BILL: I don't want you to add wood to the fire.

NAN: Then we must figure out who—

BILL: That's *my* responsibility. I'm president of the bowling league. I'm sleeping now.

[*BILL turns off lamp. NAN turns lamp on.*]

BILL: I'm sleeping in Barbara's room.

NAN: You want people talking about us sleeping apart?

BILL: Gus is our friend, okay? His bank wouldn't lend money to deaf people twenty-four years ago, and he put his reputation on the line. For *us*. For all of us. He showed *his* bank that deaf people were a good risk. He trusted us.

NAN: Sometimes I wonder.

BILL: Gus couldn't have taken that money. Good night.

[BILL turns off lamp. NAN turns on lamp.]

NAN: What if that new girl Vicki took it?

BILL: Oh, come *on!*

NAN: I don't trust her at all. . . .We could ask Gus to catch her when she deposits the money.

BILL: Jesus.

NAN: Can you ask Gus? Off the record, you know—like friends. (*Beat.*) Please?

[BILL says nothing.]

NAN: Please. Please ask Gus.

BILL: Fine. I'll see him tomorrow morning. Now could I *please* get some sleep?

[NAN gives BILL a sweet smile and then turns off lamp. Lights change to bright moonlight in the park. GUS walks by and notices a park bench. He sits down for a while. VICKI enters with an empty dog leash.]

VICKI: What are you doing here?

GUS: (*Stands up.*) Sitting. Thinking. What are you doing here?

VICKI: My dog's over there. Mind if I sit with you?

GUS: Not at all.

[VICKI sits down and looks up at the trees.]

VICKI: I love autumn. The leaves are so pretty.

GUS: (*Nods, and then watches something in the distance.*) Beautiful dog. What's his name?

VICKI: Yuki. It's Japanese for "snow."

GUS: Oh, how appropriate. How long have you had him?

VICKI: Almost five years. (*Beat.*) So . . . I've heard that you've worked at the bank for twenty-four years. Right?

GUS: (*Laughs.*) For once, a rumor's true.

VICKI: Well, I've heard lots of good things about you.

GUS: I'm shocked.

VICKI: Your friends Ida and Clovis in Kansas City have good things to say about you.

GUS: Oh, you know them, too? It's a small world. How are they doing?

VICKI: Fine. They say to pass on a warm hug to you.

[*VICKI hugs GUS.*]

GUS: (*Flushed.*) They're good people. I wish they were living here.

VICKI: Yeah, I know that feeling. There just aren't enough good deaf people around.

GUS: Yeah. Tell me about yourself.

VICKI: I guess you haven't heard the latest rumors about me.

GUS: Let me guess: You haven't earned your reputation.

VICKI: Right. (*Beat.*) We don't know anything bad about each other. That's so amazing.

GUS: Sure is. (*Chuckles.*) You've been here for a week, and you haven't heard any rumors about me? That's a real world record.

VICKI: Is it really that bad here?

GUS: Well. Let me tell you the most famous rumor about me.

[*Lights change as RUMORS #1–5 stand behind GUS and VICKI. VICKI watches GUS.*]

RUMOR #1: Hey. Did you know that Gus got promoted to vice president of his bank?

RUMOR #2: That means he'll make more money.

RUMOR #3: I wonder if he'll hire some deaf people.

RUMOR #4: I wonder if he'll buy a new BMW.

RUMOR #5: I wonder if he'll buy a huge yacht and guzzle champagne.

[*Ping. GUS looks up at VICKI.*]

GUS: I got so busy that I decided three years ago to hire this smart deaf woman named Sandra McGrosi to be the deaf community liaison/teller.

[GUS looks away. Lights back to RUMORS.]

RUMOR #1: Have you seen that new deaf girl at the bank?

RUMOR #2: Oh, that's Sandra McGrosi. She's really smart—she got a degree in finance from New York University or someplace like that.

RUMOR #3: She comes from a really strong deaf family—both parents, two brothers and three sisters, all deaf.

RUMOR #4: She seems snotty. She hasn't even shown up at the bowling alley since she moved here.

RUMOR #5: She's gorgeous, and—well-stacked.

[Ping. GUS looks up at VICKI.]

GUS: Of course, when you have only one other deaf co-worker, you two get really close. Sandra and I would tease each other, but it was nothing serious.

[GUS looks away. Lights back to RUMORS.]

RUMOR #1: I saw Gus and Sandra close to each other, carrying on. I wonder . . .

RUMOR #2: Do you know Sandra's new boyfriend? Robert Samson. Yeah, he's from Chicago, and he comes from a hearing family. I think.

RUMOR #3: Sandra and Robert's wedding was really beautiful. And Gus's toast was so touching although I couldn't understand all of his sentences.

RUMOR #4: Yeah, they're real good friends. I hear they have really nice cookouts in the backyard on weekends.

RUMOR #5: My God. Are Gus and Sandra still carrying on? I feel so awful for Darcy.

[Lights change back to "normal" as RUMORS recede. GUS looks up at VICKI.]

GUS: Later that night Sandra and Robert came over and told us to ignore those rumors. (*Beat.*) We still visit them in Chicago, but it's not the same.

VICKI: Oh, that's such a shame. How long have you been married?

GUS: A long time, and not long enough.

VICKI: Wow. Your wife's lucky.

GUS: Oh, you'll find someone special one day.

VICKI: I hope so. (*Notices her dog off in the distance; uses her voice if possible.*) Hey! Yuki! Stop digging!

GUS: Dogs don't understand what's right or wrong.

VICKI: My dog knows.

GUS: Well. I better get going. Darcy may have a dagger waiting for me if I don't get home soon. (*Beat.*) Your dog's digging a hole to China.

[*VICKI groans while GUS exits. VICKI calls her dog to come along with her as lights fade. As lights change to DARCY, GUS slips beside DARCY. She "wakes up" and turns to the audience while BILL and NAN continue sleeping.*]

DARCY: In bed Gus holds me tightly and I feel his nose breathing down my neck and the purr of his snore. After so many years we know exactly where to put our limbs around each other. (*Beat.*) At night, Gus reads his thick novels and I read my magazines. He looks so comfortable with words and numbers all around him, and I don't. (*Beat.*) All day at work I just type words into the computer, and I don't even know half of the big fancy words in the letters I type. Nan always asks me why I ever married Gus.

[*Lights change to FLASHBACK, twenty-five years ago: NAN rushes over to DARCY.*]

NAN: I just saw your new boyfriend at the bank. He looks so handsome in his suit.

DARCY: (*Radiantly.*) He's cute, isn't he.

NAN: But he's gotta learn signs faster if he's gonna marry you.

DARCY: We haven't talked much about that yet.

NAN: You're too different. He's like a *hearing* person.

DARCY: He's learning signs for me. And for my deaf friends.

NAN: Oh? And you're supposed to learn how to talk for his friends?

[Lights dim as DARCY and NAN return to their beds. Lights open on BILL "waking up."]

BILL: Night after night I find myself wondering whatever happened to the woman I loved. She used to be so full of light, so full of humor, so full of . . . warmth.

[Lights change to FLASHBACK: BILL wraps arms around NAN from behind; it is clearly more than twenty years ago.]

BILL: You can tell me.

NAN: Don't tickle me.

BILL: I can't help it. You're like a feather.

[NAN breaks away playfully from BILL.]

NAN: I'm not telling.

BILL: Just one of those itty-bitty secrets?

[NAN giggles.]

BILL: We're married now.

NAN: That's so hard to believe.

BILL: Things haven't changed.

NAN: Well, we live together. Finally.

BILL: (*Smiling.*) I know. Isn't it wonderful?

NAN: We should still do it in your car. Tonight?

BILL: You're so bad.

NAN: You can't read my mind?

BILL: Tell me.

[NAN signs very secretly in such a way that only BILL can see her. BILL glows.]

BILL: I won't tell. My kiss equals the promise.

[BILL embraces NAN, and then suddenly NAN breaks away. BILL finally turns to the audience.]

BILL: Barbara, our hearing daughter, came along, and she . . . made me feel good. I wanted to be the father I never had, and I wanted her to understand me better than I understood my own hearing father. Those years sure went by fast. (Beat.) Night after night in my dreams I find myself sleeping on a bed farther and farther away from hers, and unable to move my bed out of the room. What happened?

[As BILL "gets out of bed" and exits, NAN comes to the fore.]

NAN: In the twilight I see Barbara standing there. She looks just like yesterday when she was five years old. Her hair was so cute with white barrettes and her smile just went out to everyone who saw her. I felt so proud of her: She was *my* daughter. I walk closer and closer to her, and the closer I get to her, she grows taller and taller, and her hair changes. It is no longer long and pretty. She cuts it all off until it's short and mean. I look at her tired ears, her tired eyes, and her tired hands: Suddenly her hands, eyes, and ears are frayed and raw like old rope. (Beat.) What happened?

[Lights change. NAN scurries as if she's on the street, in the hallway of a deaf-frequented shop, and an arts & crafts club meeting. RUMORS come up to NAN at different times while GUS watches them closely.]

RUMOR #1: Did you hear what happened last night at the Alley?
NAN: I know. Isn't that awful?

[RUMOR #1 goes off. RUMOR #2 finds NAN.]

RUMOR #2: You know what else I've heard? The manager of the bowling alley took that money. I'm not surprised—he's hearing.
NAN: Oh. *That's* news.

[RUMOR #2 goes off. RUMOR #3 finds NAN.]

RUMOR #3: Seems that new girl Vicki Harp took that money.

NAN: Did she?

RUMOR #3: (*Glances around.*) Promise me you won't tell *who* told you this—

NAN: I promise.

[NAN goes off toward DARCY's office. Meanwhile other RUMORS converge on a street corner. GUS turns more antsy as he watches.]

RUMOR #1: (*To RUMOR #4.*) Seems Gus stole money from the bowling league.

RUMOR #4: That's not what I heard. I heard that this new deaf girl Vicki Happ?—Hopp?—took it.

RUMOR #2: I heard that the money totaled one thousand dollars.

RUMOR #3: No. Three thousand dollars!

RUMOR #2: Who told you that?

RUMOR #3: I don't remember.

RUMOR #5: Seems too many people saw him pocket that bowling money himself.

RUMOR #1: Who saw him?

[RUMORS look among themselves and shrug. GUS exits. Lights fade and change to DARCY's office, where DARCY is typing away on the computer. NAN flicks the light switch. DARCY turns around and hugs NAN. Meanwhile VICKI enters and watches their conversation—and later, GUS and BILL's conversation—from the shadows.]

DARCY: How did you smuggle yourself into here? Did my boss see you?

NAN: I don't think so. Is there a dorm curfew I didn't know about?

[NAN and DARCY giggle together.]

DARCY: It's funny that you mentioned our school. I was thinking about how we first met.

NAN: Oh, I know. Remember how Ms. Greyholk kept watching us in the detention room? We couldn't stop looking at each other and laughing. (*Beat.*) Oh, those days were wonderful.

DARCY: I know. (*Points to the pile of work on her desk.*) Hey—we really can't chat for long. What's up?

NAN: Well. (*Beat.*) What if Vicki stole the bowling money?

DARCY: Vicki? She just moved here. (*Beat.*) You actually came all the way here to ask me that?

NAN: This is very important—I've heard plenty of stories about her. She got engaged seven times. Imagine that!

DARCY: Are you serious?

NAN: If you hear so many stories about one person, you know there's got to be an element of truth in them somewhere.

DARCY: It's probably a recycled rumor. (*Beat.*) Why do you have to tell me gossip all the time?

NAN: You enjoy it.

DARCY: I know, but we're not living in the dorm anymore.

NAN: Hey. What's gotten into you? You never complained before.

DARCY: Gus's afraid that rumors about him will start. All over again.

NAN: Oh, everybody knows him.

DARCY: I hope so. Okay now, why don't you go home?

NAN: (*Not moving.*) I still think Vicki took the money.

DARCY: Oh, really? You have proof?

NAN: She *just* moved here, and you know that the first month after moving is always expensive.

DARCY: She wouldn't do that.

NAN: Exactly! That's why she took it.

[Lights off NAN and DARCY. Lights on GUS and BILL in GUS's office.]

BILL: Tell me: What do you think of that new girl?

GUS: She's nice.

BILL: She's pretty.

[GUS nods nonchalantly.]

BILL: I think she got the hots for me.

GUS: Really.

BILL: Do you think she got the hots for you too?

GUS: What? I only helped her out, that's all.

BILL: She looked at you. I saw her.

GUS: We're all new to her. (*Beat.*) Oh, come on. She didn't even know we were all married.

BILL: How do you know? Maybe she took the money.

GUS: I don't think so.

BILL: The deaf grapevine tells Nan that Vicki has a bad reputation.

GUS: *Who* are these people on the grapevine anyway? I mean, really?

BILL: You could check her accounts. Maybe she'll deposit our money—

GUS: She just opened a new account. (*Sighs.*) Even if she did deposit our money, I can't divulge anything.

[Lights off BILL and GUS. Lights on DARCY and NAN.]

NAN: How's Gus doing?

DARCY: He seemed a little better this morning.

NAN: Good, good.

DARCY: What's wrong?

NAN: Well, some people came up to me after you two left the bowling alley. They suspect Gus of taking the money.

DARCY: I'm not surprised.

NAN: That's why I wanted to talk with you in private: What can I do?

DARCY: Tell everyone to shut up!

NAN: I—of course I did that already.

DARCY: Did you, really?

NAN: I don't start rumors. You should know that by now.

DARCY: Do I? You've come all the way here just to . . .

NAN: We're *good* friends, remember. I trust you completely. I know anything I tell will never get out.

DARCY: Thanks. (*Beat.*) Have you heard from Barbara lately?

NAN: (*Beat.*) No.

DARCY: She'll call one day.

NAN: (*Glances around.*) I should go now.

DARCY: We'll talk more later.

[*NAN and DARCY hug, and NAN exits while DARCY goes back to her computer. Lights off DARCY. Lights on BILL and GUS.*]

BILL: Then we can't rent the bowling alley at a good price this year.

GUS: Everyone will just have to pay a little extra, that's all.

BILL: Some of these guys are living on government checks.

GUS: We can always come up with a *pro rata* plan.

BILL: What's that?

GUS: Everyone could pay the same percentage out of their annual income. The amount could vary, but the percentage would remain the same.

BILL: What? I don't understand. I can't believe your attitude—

GUS: We're not supposed to run this club like a charity.

BILL: But still—

GUS: We can call a special meeting and figure out how we can raise that money.

BILL: You make it sound like it'll be so easy.

GUS: Well, stop making it so difficult! (*Beat.*) We've been bowling there for twenty years. I can talk with the manager if you want.

BILL: I don't trust him. He's taking advantage of us.

GUS: If that's how you feel, fine. We can do something else. Do we *have* to spend the rest of our lives in the same old bowling alley?

BILL: You bored with us?

GUS: Look. I'm sorry. Okay?

[*BILL says nothing.*]

GUS: What else is there in this town? There's the deaf school, there's sports tournaments, and there's storytelling. Not much else. (*Beat.*) Can't we just enjoy ourselves in other ways?

BILL: Maybe you did steal the money, just to make us stop bowling.

GUS: What?

BILL: You could've given us a lower finance rate like the other
bank.

GUS: Wait a minute.

BILL: *You* took advantage of us.

GUS: Excuse me?

BILL: You used deaf customers to make yourself look good at the
bank.

GUS: Honestly. I'm shocked. I mean, *I* married a *deaf* woman. Are
you trying to tell me something? Or is it really Nan?

BILL: Just help us. Check all the deaf people's accounts at your
bank and see if anyone's deposited eight hundred dollars recently.

GUS: What if the thief was smart enough *not* to deposit the
money at all?

BILL: How would you know? Maybe you *do* know.

GUS: Then maybe I shouldn't have been upset about the money.

BILL: See? You're not even trying *at all* to find out who took the
bowling money. What does that say about you?

*[BILL exits. Lights off GUS. Lights dim on SPECTATORS watching a high
school football game from their bleachers; it is a chilly evening. They ad-
lib comments about certain players on the field; VICKI stands rather by
herself at one end of a row. GUS and DARCY enter. There is a slight, but
sudden, change in the air when SPECTATORS see GUS and DARCY taking their places on the bleachers. GUS and DARCY wave a hello to VICKI;
she waves back.]*

GUS: (*To SPECTATOR #1.*) The score's forty-two to six. What happened?

SPECTATOR #1: Kirby's out sick tonight.

GUS: Nothing like a star player out of commission.

SPECTATOR #1: I don't understand.

GUS: The team's losing because Kirby always carries the team, and he's not on the team tonight.
SPECTATOR #1: I see.

[*Other SPECTATORS ad-lib with smallish signs about GUS while GUS and DARCY continue watching the game. VICKI and GUS trade warm glances.*]

SPECTATOR #2: (*Sotto voce.*) See that guy over there? He's a thief.
SPECTATOR #3: (*Sotto voce.*) Oh, I know. I don't know how Darcy puts up with him.
SPECTATOR #4: (*Sotto voce.*) He's real greedy. Why else work in a bank?

[*At that moment, GUS happens to turn and catches SPECTATOR #4's remark. He reveals nothing, and turns back to the game.*]

DARCY: You all right?
GUS: It's nothing.
SPECTATOR #5: (*To SPECTATOR #4.*) Gus's just a big-headed oralist who wants to rule the deaf world.

[*Just at that moment GUS turns around and catches the frozen look on SPECTATOR #5's face.*]

GUS: You talking about me?
SPECTATOR #5: No. No.
GUS: I'm an oralist trying to *rule* the deaf world?
DARCY: Stop. Just leave them alone.

[*All SPECTATORS are watching GUS instead of the game.*]

GUS: What if I said *you* were one of those deafies trying to rule the hearing world?
SPECTATOR #5: Yes. That's got to happen.
GUS: Then hearies will say we've oppressed them like they oppressed us. (*Beat.*) Two wrongs don't make a right.
DARCY: Stop. Please—
GUS: Why don't you stop talking about me and start *doing* something useful? Like supporting your own leaders?

SPECTATOR #5: You didn't have to take that money.

GUS: I *didn't* take the money!

DARCY: (*To SPECTATOR #5.*) Where's your proof?

SPECTATOR #5: He lied to everybody before.

GUS: I never slept with Sandra, okay?

DARCY: She even told me herself.

SPECTATOR #4: (*To SPECTATOR #5.*) Just leave them alone.

GUS: Thank you. (*To DARCY.*) Why should I waste my time here with people gossiping behind my back? I'm going home.

DARCY: Wait—

[But GUS is already gone, and DARCY follows. VICKI turns to SPEC-TATORS and gives them a disgusted glare as lights fade. Lights change to night—approximately the same time the night before at the park. GUS is sitting alone on the bench. VICKI hesitates toward GUS and sits down on the bench. BILL hovers from the shadows, watching VICKI in particular.]

VICKI: I was very surprised you called.

GUS: You looked so beautiful at the game tonight. (*Beat.*) Actually, I thought about you all day.

VICKI: Me too. Those people really embarrass me sometimes. (*Beat.*) How's Darcy?

GUS: She's fine.

VICKI: Well, the big news at my school was *who* stole the money.

GUS: Don't tell me your *students* know about this.

VICKI: Well. Yes.

GUS: Oh, great. Next thing I'll hear is some TV broadcaster announcing to the world: "Angus Edward Horton, vice president of the Walnut National Bank, has been accused of stealing eight hundred dollars from the Lansel Deaf Bowling League. More details to follow at eleven."

[VICKI laughs in spite of herself.]

GUS: It's not exactly funny . . .

VICKI: I know, I know. (*Beat.*) Does your wife know you're here with me?

GUS: (*Beat.*) No. I told her I needed to take a walk.
VICKI: You're still upset.

[*VICKI pats GUS's lap.*]

VICKI: You can't run away from these rumors.
GUS: I'm not running. . . . (*A long beat.*) My life might be easier if I divorced my wife and married a hearing woman who thinks deafness is a sin.

[*VICKI bursts out laughing.*]

GUS: Darcy doesn't always understand this kind of humor.
VICKI: You shouldn't look down on her. She's a good woman.
GUS: Oh, I love her. And I don't look down on her. It's just that I feel so *good* talking with you.
VICKI: Who do you think took the money?
GUS: Oh, I have no idea. I just wish it was over, closed.
VICKI: It won't go away.
GUS: I know, I know. (*Beat; smiles.*) What about *you*?
VICKI: What?
GUS: Did *you* steal the money?
VICKI: Whatever gave you that idea?
GUS: Guess who.
VICKI: That bitch!
GUS: Nan doesn't know what she's doing. She's a good person, really. Deep down.
VICKI: Must be *very* deep down. I find it hard to believe.
GUS: People do change.

[*VICKI looks at GUS quietly.*]

VICKI: Why aren't there more deaf men like you?
GUS: That's funny. I look at my wife and wish that there were more people like her.

[*Lights fade as BILL walks off with glances back at VICKI. Lights change to morning. VICKI is on her way to work; she carries a knapsack. BILL, from the opposite direction, carries the day's newspaper. NAN watches them like a hawk from her kitchen window.*]

VICKI: Good morning to you.

BILL: Good morning to you, too.

VICKI: Did anyone find the money yet?

BILL: No. How did you get home that night?

VICKI: I got a ride home. With the Gansons.

BILL: What time did you leave?

VICKI: Right after Gus and Darcy left. Why are you asking me all these questions? I'm not under suspicion, am I?

BILL: I have to suspect everyone.

VICKI: Well, I don't want this to affect my *new* job. (*Beat.*) I hope you believe that people do tell the truth once in a while. Who else have you asked?

BILL: No one.

VICKI: Oh. So you've already decided that I'm guilty because of my "reputation"?

BILL: I didn't mean that.

VICKI: I'm waiting for someone to accuse *you* of taking the money.

BILL: Me?

VICKI: Just because you're the president of the bowling league doesn't mean you're not guilty.

BILL: You think *I* took the money? You don't know me.

VICKI: You don't know me, either.

BILL: (*Beat.*) You're right. I apologize. It's just so hard to investigate friends.

VICKI: I can imagine. There's no trust anymore. (*Beat.*) I hope *we* can become friends.

BILL: (*Considers the possibility.*) Nan wouldn't like it.

VICKI: (*Smiles.*) I understand.

BILL: No, you don't.

VICKI: What's there to understand? It's pretty obvious.

BILL: What's obvious?

VICKI: Nan doesn't trust you enough.

BILL: No—yes—well, no.

VICKI: Am I bothering you?

BILL: No, no.

VICKI: Good, Bill. (*Beat.*) I have to go to work.

BILL: Wait—I'm curious. Have you heard things about me?

VICKI: If I wanted to know, I'd ask you myself.

BILL: I sure wish more people would do that. I get so tired of all this stupid gossip.

VICKI: Oh, me too. So let's agree to ignore it. And *anyone* who spreads it.

[VICKI goes off while BILL says nothing. Lights fade to GUS walking onstage and shaking his hand with his imaginary boss and nods for his imaginary interpreter to begin.]

GUS: Good morning, sir. How are you? (*Beat.*) Good, good. (*Nods and chuckles.*) Pardon me? What letter?

[GUS accepts the imaginary letter from his boss. As GUS reads it, the RUMORS come onstage behind GUS. Their lines should be delivered with a rapid-fire precision while GUS turns livid from reading the letter.]

RUMOR #1: Dear Mr. Hendricks—

RUMOR #2: We is [*sic*] sorry that Gus Horton—

RUMOR #3: May be guilty of stealing money ($1000.)—

RUMOR #4: From my (*Gestures at the word being "xxx" out.*) our bowling league.

RUMOR #5: Check out please Gus's records—

RUMOR #1: And other deaf people's too.

RUMOR #2: We deaf are not sure if we should trust Gus—

RUMOR #3: Even if he worked [*sic*] at your bank.

RUMOR #4: Thank you very much.

RUMOR #5: Period.

[GUS steps downstage.]

GUS: I can't believe this!

[Lights BLACKOUT.]

END OF ACT ONE.

ACT TWO

[Lights open as GUS paces the stage with the imaginary letter in his hand, and then finally turns to BILL, who's just stepped into the neutral space between both households.]

GUS: Did Nan do this? *(Thrusts the letter to BILL.)*
BILL: I don't understand. Let me see.

[As BILL turns to the Rozwell household, lights go on NAN standing. (GUS and NAN do not address each other at all in this scene; they talk directly to BILL only.)]

BILL: *(To NAN.)* Did you write a letter to Gus's bank president?
NAN: What letter?
BILL: Someone wrote an anonymous letter. *(To GUS.)* Why would Nan write such a letter?
GUS: Nan doesn't like me. She never tries to talk to me.
BILL: But that's not enough reason. *(To NAN.)* Gus thinks you wrote it.
NAN: I can't believe he'd think that about me. My English is so lousy, I'd never write anything.
BILL: He thinks a deaf person wrote it.
NAN: I'm not the only deaf person in town. Hearing people don't always have good English, either, you know.
BILL: Then who could've written this? *(To GUS.)* You can't accuse *my* wife.
GUS: Do you trust her completely?

[BILL says nothing. Then:]

BILL: *(To NAN.)* He doesn't trust you.
NAN: He always thinks that the deaf community should be one way and it's not. He doesn't trust *them.*
BILL: He's just upset, that's all. *(To GUS.)* What did your boss say?
GUS: He was not very pleased. *I'm* not very pleased. There's no proof I took the money.
BILL: I'm not happy either. *(To NAN.)* I'm disgusted too.

NAN: What if Gus wrote the letter himself?

BILL: *What? (To GUS.)*

GUS: I don't know why I even bothered to fight for deaf rights at my bank in the first place.

BILL: We appreciate the work you've done. We all do. (*To NAN.*) Why would you think that?

NAN: Maybe he wants to make it look like someone else took the money.

BILL: You've just decided that?

NAN: What about him? He just did the same thing.

GUS: If this continues, I don't know what I'll do next.

NAN: Gus has really twisted you around. I can't believe *you* didn't stop him from turning against your own wife.

BILL: I had to let him blow off steam, okay?

GUS: I'm going to ask the police to investigate this letter.

BILL: Are we really working together to solve the money problem?

GUS: I have no choice now.

NAN: Maybe you're making up the letter. You're trying to catch me. *I* didn't take the money.

BILL: I didn't make the letter up. Gus showed me the letter.

GUS: Maybe you should ask Nan. See how she reacts.

NAN: Oh, he's looking for someone to blame, and you want me put away.

BILL: I get enough excitement here in this house.

GUS: Only a sick person would do this.

NAN: Maybe he really wants to make deaf people look bad so he can look good.

GUS: Excuse me. I'm going to the police now.

NAN: He thinks he's so high and mighty. Well, he's not!

GUS: Whoever wrote this letter is a real coward. No name, no signature, nothing!

[NAN and GUS exits while BILL shakes his head wearily. Lights change to DARCY and GUS in their kitchen.]

DARCY: I can't believe that. (*Looks at the letter.*)

GUS: Who else?

DARCY: But you can't start pointing fingers now.

GUS: The police said that the letter didn't come from a computer. Do you know anyone with an IBM Selectric II?

DARCY: Well, Nan doesn't have a typewriter.

GUS: How do you know?

DARCY: She'd never write a letter like that. She's too embarrassed by her English.

GUS: Who else, then?

DARCY: Did you ask Bill himself?

GUS: No. This letter—oh, why can't people just leave me alone? I'm just so disgusted.

DARCY: That's just them.

GUS: I can't believe *you* sometimes. That a smart and classy woman like you would still defend these people.

DARCY: They're a part of me, okay? Remember the things you used to say?

[Lights change. RUMORS are now GUS at various points in his earlier relationship with DARCY; they speak directly to DARCY. GUS tries to interrupt each RUMOR in some way each time by talking to DARCY as well.]

RUMOR #1: Why do these people have to embarrass me all the time? They even asked me about what time we go to bed.

GUS: They haven't picked up all the social mores of a hearing person because they're deaf.

RUMOR #2: Maybe I haven't accepted myself.

GUS: What? I don't hide the fact that I'm hard of hearing. What more do you want?

RUMOR #3: I'm not looking down on our deaf community.

GUS: *Our* community? I'll never be fully accepted. Just because I've married you doesn't mean that it's my community too.

RUMOR #4: Why do they have to keep testing me all the time? One little mistake, and I'm thrown out on the street.

GUS: They're just jealous. They don't like my brains, period.

RUMOR #5: Why can't *everybody* work together for deaf rights?

GUS: You can only speak for yourself. That's all I know.

[Lights change. RUMORS recede, as GUS sighs.]

DARCY: You've changed.

GUS: Well, there's nothing definite about being deaf in America now. Hearing people have always screwed us over. And *we* keep misunderstanding and squashing each other.

DARCY: Great! Since you're such a genius, tell us how we can be one big happy family.

GUS: (*Beat; sadly.*) I wish I knew. I really do. Everybody seems to have all the answers, but no one agrees on a single one. Oh, I don't know. (*Beat.*) We've got to stop wasting our time in the deaf community. They do nothing but backstab each other.

DARCY: Hearing people are no better.

GUS: There are more hearing people to pick from. Easy.

DARCY: Nan keeps asking me why I picked you in the first place.

GUS: Does she? I should kick her all the way to hell!

DARCY: Then you'll have to kick me right along with her.

[DARCY scurries off. Lights change to VICKI, wandering aimlessly yet happily all over the stage. GUS sits to one side and looks away while BILL watches VICKI; both men stay in the shadows.]

VICKI: I heard the most beautiful rumor of all: Vicki's in love. For the longest time she'd thought love was an empty word. She woke up earlier each morning just to catch the first rays, and she was happy to sit and cover herself with a blanket on the porch swing and watch the cars go by. She felt warm as the frost melted slowly, and the grass soon stopped shining with cold. There, in her dreams, Gus would stand tall as he gives her a sweet kiss under an oak tree. They would simply hold each other without saying a word for hours at a time. His hands would be sinewy and strong, and his eyes would shimmer like a bubbly brook. In that embrace, she'd feel the sunlight change from crispness to a familiar warmth. There, on the porch, she was happy to wait all day for the man she loved, but even in that waiting she couldn't concentrate on the book she was reading. For her books weren't enough; she yearned to be a romance heroine herself. Now I've heard she's come to the end of *her* romance novel: Her fantasy is about to become nonfiction.

[As lights fade, VICKI wanders dreamily offstage. BILL looks on, heartbroken. GUS goes off. Lights open on NAN and a few imaginary players already in their first round of bridge. DARCY arrives.]

NAN: (*To imaginary players.*) Excuse me. (*Opens the front door.*) I'm surprised you're here so early.

DARCY: Well, actually, I was a little bored.

NAN: You can sit there.

DARCY: Thanks. (*To imaginary player.*) How are you doing? (*Beat.*) Great. How's your daughter doing? Yale? Next year? Wow. (*Beat.*) Congratulations.

NAN: See? I always told you that girl would go far.

DARCY: (*To another player.*) How's your husband doing? (*Beat.*) Laid off? I'm sorry. Are you all right with money? (*Beat.*) You two can come over to my house for dinner. Save a little money once in a while. (*Stops.*) Did I say something wrong? (*Beat.*) So you think Gus is a thief too?

NAN: I warned you before. We *have* to find who took it.

DARCY: (*To PLAYERS.*) I want to know what else you've all heard.

NAN: You know I don't believe them, of course.

DARCY: Tell me. I just want to see how bad it's gotten.

[Lights off DARCY and NAN. Lights on VICKI and GUS, in the park that evening.]

GUS: At least we didn't meet in private. We have to show we have nothing to hide. What's the latest dirt on me?

VICKI: I've heard the most vicious things about you all day . . .

GUS: Come on. Tell me.

VICKI: Take your pick: You were fired from your job *and* you were forced to resign *and* you were in jail.

GUS: Not a pretty menu, isn't it?

[*VICKI laughs.*]

VICKI: I'm so glad to see you.

GUS: Me too.

VICKI: Where's Darcy?

GUS: We had a fight. I think she went off to Nan's.

VICKI: What happened?

GUS: I lost my temper.

VICKI: Is it true that someone wrote a letter about you at the bank?

GUS: Yes. I could lose my job.

VICKI: But no proof, right? They can't fire you. Not after twenty-four years.

GUS: I wish my wife wasn't so close to Nan. She's such a gossip.

VICKI: Gossips make lousy friends. I think your wife's afraid.

GUS: Afraid of what?

VICKI: Nan has power here in this town because of fear. It's no secret that she loves to gossip, and you don't want anyone talking about you. So you have to be nice to these people. That's fear.

GUS: No, no. They have a real friendship from years ago.

VICKI: Oops. Guess I was wrong.

GUS: Nice try, though. (*Beat.*) Guess I'm just not deaf enough for my wife.

[*Lights off GUS and VICKI. Lights on DARCY and NAN.*]

NAN: Typewriter? Whatever for?

DARCY: You know.

NAN: Honest. I don't know what you're talking about.

DARCY: Letter.

NAN: Oh. You mean Gus's letter of resignation?

DARCY: That's how bad the lies have gotten? (*Beat.*) Fact: Gus has not resigned from his job.

NAN: Too late. Once they're out, rumors belong to everyone and people do with them whatever they want.

DARCY: Someone sent my husband's boss an anonymous letter about the bowling money. Did *you* write it?

NAN: I can't believe you'd suspect me.

DARCY: I've also heard you suspected Gus of stealing the money. Why can't I suspect you too?

NAN: You can search my entire house. There's no typewriter here. Honest.

DARCY: (*Beat.*) Okay. I believe you. (*Beat.*) What have you heard about Gus lately?

NAN: Many stories. Way too many Gus stories.

DARCY: I'm his wife. I should know.

NAN: But I'm not Rumor Central.

[Lights off DARCY and NAN. Lights on GUS and VICKI. BILL watches their conversation from the shadows.]

VICKI: (*Sighs.*) You're handsomer than ever. And have I got a nice rumor for you.

GUS: Oh. What?

[VICKI comes closer to GUS.]

VICKI: I'm in love.

GUS: I . . .

VICKI: I've never been able to talk so well and so clearly as I have with you. All the other deaf men I've met don't even begin to compare with you. I'm tired of being a trophy on other men's walls.

[VICKI and GUS look at each other with tenderness. GUS slowly moves away.]

VICKI: Am I doing something wrong?

GUS: No. Well, yes. It's just that . . .

VICKI: I feel good too.

GUS: Yeah. It's been a while.

VICKI: It's okay.

GUS: I . . .

VICKI: If you want more privacy, my house is right over there.

GUS: No. Too many eyes all over the place.

[*Lights off GUS and VICKI. Lights on DARCY and NAN.*]

DARCY: Tell me every single Gus story you've heard in the last few days.

NAN: That'd take me hours. We'd still be up until sunrise.

DARCY: What's the worst rumor you've heard about Gus?

NAN: (*Beat.*) We're really good friends, are we?

[*DARCY nods slowly.*]

NAN: Three people told me they saw Gus and Vicki carrying on in the park at night. Seems they're having an affair.

DARCY: (*Beat.*) Oh, please.

NAN: Honest.

DARCY: That's got to be a lie.

NAN: Well, that one happens to be true.

DARCY: He wouldn't do that to me.

NAN: Ask David Kemp or Iris Showsky or Marie Bowman. Those are the three people who saw her talking with Gus. On the bench.

[*DARCY walks around in a daze.*]

DARCY: He wouldn't do that to me. He wouldn't.

NAN: Believe me. I was shocked at first.

DARCY: I'm going to ask him. Right now.

NAN: Wait . . .

[*But DARCY is already gone. Lights off DARCY and NAN. Lights on GUS and VICKI.*]

VICKI: I'd never tell anyone.

GUS: You know how people will talk.

VICKI: Oh, let them.

GUS: I have a reputation. And a wife.

VICKI: You can divorce her.

GUS: Then I could divorce you too.

VICKI: That won't happen.

GUS: People won't think well of me.

VICKI: Everyone respects you.

[GUS raises his eyebrows and says nothing. VICKI touches GUS.]

GUS: *(Finally; not looking at VICKI.)* I'm sorry.

VICKI: There's nothing to be sorry about.

GUS: *(Interrupts brusquely.)* I just can't do it.

[VICKI stops. She glances around and sits down. GUS finally sits next to her.]

GUS: We can still be friends.

VICKI: *(Finally.)* Yes.

GUS: But we can't meet like this anymore.

VICKI: I understand. *(Beat.)* How can you live in this town for so long?

GUS: Living with someone who knows me and loves me and trusts me no matter what people say really helps. *(Beat.)* I'm sorry.

[GUS sighs and exits. BILL wants very much to approach VICKI, but he notices the RUMORS eyeing him, daring him to step out of the shadows. BILL doesn't, and exits.]

VICKI: *(Pause; sadly to where GUS has gone.)* I'll just dream a little dream of you, and pray for a real dream that will come true.

[Lights fade off VICKI, and lights on the Horton household. Lights on NAN sitting by herself. BILL arrives.]

NAN: What took you so long? I was waiting for you. All the bridge players left already.

BILL: I'm sorry. It was just traffic.

NAN: Looking for Vicki?

BILL: Whoa. Where did you get that idea—

NAN: I saw you talking with her this morning.

BILL: What are you, a spy?

NAN: I happened to look out the window. There you were.

BILL: Great. You can tell me how to cheat.

NAN: You trying to make fun of me?

BILL: That was the first time Vicki and I were alone together.

NAN: You were planning to see that girl tonight.

BILL: Are you gonna lie to everyone about Vicki and me?

NAN: I don't start rumors. I collect them.

BILL: For what?

NAN: It's better than books.

BILL: (*Beat.*) I'm not happy with you.

NAN: Then those stories about Vicki are indeed true.

BILL: She's someone I'd trust. More than you.

NAN: She's young. She's got a lot to learn.

BILL: What if Vicki and I did fall in love?

[NAN stops and holds her breath.]

BILL: What if we did fall in love with each other?

NAN: She wouldn't be that stupid. (*Beat.*) She's having an affair with Gus.

BILL: He wouldn't do that.

NAN: She has a way with married men, it seems.

BILL: Who told you?

NAN: Three people.

BILL: All liars?

NAN: Three *different* people told me.

BILL: I don't believe you. (*Beat.*) Does Darcy know?

NAN: I told her just now.

BILL: Don't be so stupid.

NAN: The wife shouldn't be the last to know! (*Beat.*) And as for you, I intend to be the *first* to know!

BILL: I only said: What if Vicki and I fell in love?

NAN: I don't like those what-ifs.

BILL: You do. Oh, you sure do.

NAN: What? What are you talking about?

BILL: Gossip. It's not any different from what-ifs.

NAN: Well, it's got more truth than what-ifs.

BILL: That doesn't mean anything.

NAN: (*Beat.*) You don't want me anymore.

BILL: I'm still married to you.

NAN: You don't smile much anymore.

BILL: Thanks for the weather report.

NAN: We used to tease each other all the time.

BILL: You know why. I'm going to bed.

NAN: Whatever for? You haven't had dinner yet.

BILL: I'm not hungry.

NAN: People will wonder about us.

BILL: They're already wondering why *I'm* still married to you. What's the difference?

NAN: You can't spend any more time with Vicki.

BILL: What if I want to? She seems like someone I could trust.

NAN: You can't trust this town.

BILL: Your *mouth* runs this town.

[*BILL exits as NAN looks after him. Lights change. DARCY enters the Horton household and looks all over for GUS. Not there.*]

DARCY: Oooh, he's finished!

[*GUS happens to enter.*]

DARCY: Where have you been?

GUS: Walking.

DARCY: Oh, really?

GUS: I needed to cool off. That letter really upset me.

DARCY: Where were you? In the park? With Vicki?

GUS: Unh, yes. It's not what you think it is. I mean, we're just friends.

DARCY: Just "friends"?

GUS: Come on now.

DARCY: Why else would you take those late-night walks?

GUS: That was never my plan. Not at first.

DARCY: Oh, one thing led to another, and now you're writhing around in Vicki's bed.

GUS: Wait. Wait—

DARCY: Seems Nan's right. I thought those stories about Vicki were lies. Not anymore.

GUS: Stop. Stop and think about this—doesn't this remind you of those Sandra stories?

DARCY: Yes. And why is it happening again? Don't you lie to me.

GUS: I'm not.

DARCY: Well?

GUS: Vicki and I did meet. Three times, okay?

DARCY: Oh, you jerk.

GUS: Let me finish. ———————————————

DARCY: Now I can't trust you anymore.

[GUS grabs DARCY by the arms and forces her to look at him.]

GUS: Please. Look. Vicki and I did meet three times, but we never, *never* did it.

DARCY: Exactly what were you doing with Vicki?

GUS: She needed company.

DARCY: And I don't? You had to go off and take long walks just to talk . . . ?

GUS: We talked. That's it.

DARCY: "That's it"?

GUS: I kept thinking about you. I came home.

DARCY: Are you going to stop thinking about her?

GUS: That's all over. I want to be with you for the rest of my life.

DARCY: How would I know you'll never see her again?

GUS: Please . . . look at me.

DARCY: How can I if you keep looking at other women?

GUS: I only looked at *one* and didn't even kiss her, let alone go to bed with her.

DARCY: You shouldn't have met with her in the first place. Why did you spend time with her? Why not me?

GUS: I just needed to talk with *someone.*

DARCY: You prefer Vicki because I'm not as well-read or witty as you. She works in a library, so she knows a lot more than I do.

GUS: Reading books doesn't mean anything. You have more common sense than I do.

DARCY: That's right. You're not thinking clearly because of your dick!

GUS: I just needed to talk with someone *outside* all of these rumors, okay! God, I wish I was never involved in *anything* in the first place.

DARCY: People keep asking if you took the money. Did you?

GUS: (*Stops.*) I can't believe you actually asked me that.

DARCY: That's right. I don't know who to believe anymore.

[*DARCY runs offstage as lights fade. Lights open on CUSTOMERS entering the bank. GUS stands on one side of the stage, and the five CUSTOMERS are standing in line.*]

GUS: (*Behind the imaginary counter.*) Good morning! What can I do for you?

CUSTOMER #1: I'd like to close my account.

GUS: Oh. Okay. (*Pulls out a special form and inserts it into the machine.*) Check or cash?

CUSTOMER #1: Check.

GUS: One moment. (*Taps some keys onto his computer.*) The check will be ready in a few minutes. Could you wait to the side so I can help the next customer?

[*CUSTOMER #1 nods slowly and stands to the side as CUSTOMER #2 steps up.*]

GUS: Good morning. What can I do for you?

CUSTOMER #2: I want to withdraw all my money from this bank.

GUS: I see. Check or cash?

CUSTOMER #2: Check. It's safer.

GUS: Just a moment. (*Taps some keys on his computer.*) Your check will be ready in a minute. Could you move to the side so I can help the next customer?

[*CUSTOMER #2 steps to the side as CUSTOMER #3 steps up.*]

GUS: How can I help you?

CUSTOMER #3: Check.

GUS: All of it?

CUSTOMER #3: Yes.

GUS: Just a moment, please. (*Taps some keys into his computer.*) If the three of you could move over to the side, all of your checks will be ready in a few minutes.

[*CUSTOMER #3 joins CUSTOMERS #1 and #2 as CUSTOMER #4 steps up.*]

CUSTOMER #4: Check.

GUS: You, too?

[*CUSTOMER #4 nods.*]

GUS: Your check will be ready in a few minutes. (*Taps some keys into his computer.*) Please move over.

[*CUSTOMER #4 joins the other three CUSTOMERS as CUSTOMER #5 steps up. GUS looks up to see his imaginary boss.*]

GUS: (*To CUSTOMER #5.*) Excuse me. (*To Boss.*) Oh. They all want to close their accounts. (*Beat.*) I'm not sure why, Mr. Hendricks. (*Nods.*) I'm working on it. (*Sighs.*) Yes, sir. Thanks. (*To RUMOR #5.*) How can I help you?

RUMOR #5: You plan to steal my money too?

GUS: Check or cash?

RUMOR #5: I don't want you to touch my money again.

[*GUS looks at the other RUMORS.*]

GUS: (*To RUMOR #5.*) Thank you for your patience.

[*As GUS continues to tear the checks from the printer, he looks ready to kill someone.*

Lights fade to DARCY, BILL, and NAN trying to sleep, but only in fits. NAN sighs and gets out of her bed; she puts on her jacket and goes outside in the park. BILL merely turns over to sleep some more. NAN is alone.]

NAN: The winds above me cleanse the dark skies and the world suddenly looks like a huge spider web: Telephone lines string each house to the next, until the flax of words choke the next victim within hours, days, weeks, sometimes years. Between our hands we weave a far more lethal web, a sticky trap of mere words and accusations; we are no longer stupid little flies waiting to get caught. We are also spiders in waiting. (*Beat*.) Moonlight cuts through the leaves, and the world looks a pale blue—oh, look at my hands. They've gotten so cold!

[NAN exits. Lights change to GUS, going through the motions of readying himself for the day. GUS, satisfied, picks up his briefcase, about to exit the house when he realizes something.]

GUS: Damn. I'm not supposed to go to work today.

[GUS puts down his briefcase. BILL rings the bell. GUS looks out the window.]

GUS: (*To himself.*) Oh, great. Now I'll end up in jail.

[GUS opens the door.]

BILL: Good morning. May I come in?
GUS: Yeah. What do you want?
BILL: I heard what happened yesterday. These people were really mean to take their money out.
GUS: Thanks. (*Beat.*) I was actually worried that I'd find you and Nan at the end of the line.
BILL: Oh, don't worry. We're *your* friends. Like always.
GUS: I've been asked to take a leave-of-absence for a few weeks. You know what that means? It means the bank doesn't trust me anymore. I could get demoted. Maybe fired.
BILL: I came here to tell you that Nan and I are *not* closing our accounts at your bank.
GUS: I really appreciate that. Thanks.
BILL: I also went to talk with the manager at the Alley this morning, but the place was closed for renovations.

GUS: Maybe that place should stay closed. Permanently.

BILL: Any news on the letter?

GUS: No. (*Beat.*) It's a terrible feeling that I have—that I can't just trust any deaf person.

BILL: But you trust me. Do you?

GUS: Your wife. I can't.

BILL: I know.

[*Meanwhile NAN presses the doorbell to the Horton household. Lights flash. GUS walks to the door and finds NAN. BILL sees her.*]

BILL: You following me or what?

NAN: You aren't supposed to be here. Go to work. *(To GUS.)* You, too.

GUS: Oh, for once you haven't heard the latest.

NAN: What?

BILL: You better go. I'll explain later.

NAN: No. Where's Darcy?

GUS: Somewhere in the house. She's not talking to me. Thank you so much for your "friendship."

BILL: Wait a minute. What happened?

NAN: I only told her what I heard.

BILL: And what was that?

GUS: She *thought* I was having an affair with Vicki Harp.

BILL: (*To NAN.*) Oh, did you?

NAN: Remember I warned you about that girl.

BILL: That's enough.

NAN: I didn't make that up. (*To GUS.*) Three people saw you and Vicki together in the park.

GUS: Get out of my house!

NAN: I came to see Darcy.

[*DARCY enters. NAN moves past GUS and BILL to embrace her.*]

NAN: How are you doing?

DARCY: Better.

NAN: I'm so happy to hear that.

GUS: Happy that there's more dirty laundry for you to wash?

DARCY: (*To BILL.*) Can you leave?

BILL: Me?

NAN: We can go upstairs and talk.

GUS: Oh, no. (*To DARCY.*) You've got to stop listening to other people and listen to yourself. Inside where there's truth.

NAN: Now you're getting too "hearing."

GUS: Oh no, no. How is it possible that you could be given this . . . power to decide who's acceptable and who's not around here? What gave you the right to decide whether I'm guilty or not? What gave you the right to lie about other people? Huh?

[DARCY tries to stop GUS, but—]

GUS: I thought if I was nice and diplomatic, I'd earn everyone's respect but no, it seems I'm wrong. Deeply wrong. It seems that if I want to get ahead in this world, I have to be as scheming as you. I've worked for twenty-four years to get to where I am and you've only worked one hour to blow it all away.

DARCY: Stop—

GUS: I'm not finished! (*To NAN.*) I have no proof, but I know *you* wrote the letter. You're a real coward.

NAN: Coward? You wouldn't even look into everyone's accounts.

GUS: Is that why you decided that I'm guilty? Fine. Prove it!

NAN: I've never accused you of anything.

GUS: Maybe not directly—

DARCY: Please stop—

BILL: (*To NAN.*) Please. Don't get him so angry.

NAN: (*To GUS.*) You calling me a liar?

GUS: Yes.

NAN: I didn't write that letter. What would I get out of it? (*Beat.*) I didn't start any of those stories about you.

GUS: You're lucky that rumors have no name tags.

DARCY: (*To BILL and NAN.*) Maybe you two should go home.

NAN: (*To DARCY.*) Don't you need some support?

GUS: How can you help her? Give her a hug? Easy. A patient ear? No problem. But trust? Darcy can figure that one out.

[DARCY sighs.]

NAN: We know each other too well.

GUS: Fine! *(Turns to DARCY and looks at her for a moment.)* I've decided this much: You have two choices now—me or Nan.

[GUS turns and goes off. DARCY looks after him as the doorbell flashes. It is VICKI. BILL answers it.]

VICKI: What are you doing here?

BILL: You've come at a bad time.

VICKI: I need to talk to Darcy.

BILL: *(Turns to DARCY.)* Vicki wants to talk to you.

NAN: The nerve! I could just kill that bitch.

DARCY: Tell her to stay away from Gus. My husband.

[BILL goes back to the door.]

BILL: Please stay away from Gus.

VICKI: I really want to stop a new and ugly story about me. *(Beat.)* Please?

[BILL sighs and opens the door.]

NAN: *(To BILL.)* Hey. What are you doing?

VICKI: Thank you. *(Enters and sees NAN.)* I'm not surprised *you're* here.

DARCY: Don't waste your time here.

NAN: How dare you embarrass my best friend like this?

DARCY: Put your nose back where it belongs—in books.

NAN: Why don't you marry a hearing man? You need a real challenge.

BILL: *(Tries to pull NAN to the front door.)* Come on, come on.

NAN: Leave me alone.

DARCY: *(To VICKI.)* I have nothing else to say to you.

VICKI: Will you listen to me, please?

DARCY: You want my opinion? I should've listened to Nan all along.

VICKI: You're right. Nan really knows it all.

BILL: (*To NAN.*) We should leave them alone.

VICKI: She's hungry for new tidbits. That's why she won't leave.

NAN: I'm here for Darcy and no one else.

VICKI: I wish I had a friend just like you.

BILL: Come on. *Come on.*

NAN: (*To VICKI.*) You trying to be "hearing" like Gus? No wonder you two are perfect for each other.

DARCY: Will you please shut up? (*To VICKI.*) You better say whatever you want to say fast.

[*NAN is about to say something but BILL restrains her.*]

VICKI: Some people told me they'd heard about Gus and me. I only wanted *you* to know that Gus and I never slept together.

NAN: Next I'll hear that you and Gus ran off to Las Vegas.

VICKI: (*To DARCY.*) What kind of a friend is Nan if she doesn't listen to anyone?

DARCY: Shut up!

NAN: I'm her best friend.

VICKI: Maybe I should sign up for a course under you and learn how to keep chattering all day.

NAN: Oooh, you think you're so witty. Well, you're not.

BILL: I give up. I'm going upstairs and talk with Gus.

[*BILL goes off.*]

VICKI: Gus is here? He's not working?

DARCY: You're not going near him.

NAN: It's all your fault.

VICKI: What?

DARCY: Get out.

VICKI: Please believe me. Nothing happened. We had some nice talks.

[*GUS and BILL return.*]

GUS: (*To VICKI.*) What are you doing here?

VICKI: Telling the truth.

[DARCY moves GUS away from VICKI.]

GUS: Doesn't anyone believe her? And me? We never slept together.

VICKI: Why can't you believe him? It's really sad that no one trusts each other. *(To DARCY.)* You don't even believe your own husband.

DARCY: She has a reputation.

GUS: Is any reputation perfect? No one's perfect. *(Beat.)* What else can I say to change your mind?

[DARCY looks at GUS, and then GUS moves a distance away from them.]

NAN: He's asking for a pity party.

BILL: *(To VICKI and NAN.)* Let's leave.

NAN: *(To VICKI.)* If you want to change your reputation, you should stop dating men all the time.

VICKI: Like your daughter?

NAN: Where did you hear that?

[VICKI shrugs.]

NAN: Who told you?

[VICKI shrugs again.]

NAN: *(To DARCY.)* Did *you* tell anyone? Gus?

DARCY: Of course not.

NAN: *(To BILL.)* Did you tell anyone?

[BILL shakes his head no.]

NAN: I know you did. Who else?

BILL: Oh, damn you! I don't care if Barbara's a dyke. I don't even care if the whole world knows. It doesn't matter to me anymore. You drove my Barbara away, you drove my friends away, and you're just about to drive me away! I am a lonely father who really, really loves Barbara. I miss her like hell. Thanks to you!

NAN: She didn't want to be with us. Just like hearing people.

BILL: She got tired of *you* talking about other people.

NAN: Everybody talks about other people.

BILL: But why do *you* have to spread stories? What makes you the way you are? *(Beat.)* You always complained of hearing people oppressing you; *you're* no better. You squashed Barbara. And me. I'm fed up.

NAN: Don't go—

[The doorbell flashes. DARCY answers the front door. She tries to understand the hearing manager's gestures and accepts a package from him.]

DARCY: *(Uses voice, if possible.)* Oh, thank you. *(Checks the package.)* Thank you! *(Rushes to hug the manager warmly.)*

[DARCY closes the door, and turns to BILL and NAN.]

DARCY: Seems the manager found the money when they were tearing out the old benches.

[DARCY looks at GUS, who then accepts the package. He then gives NAN a cold stare. VICKI looks at BILL and NAN, then exits quietly. NAN and BILL are left alone. BILL moves to leave the Horton house. NAN intercepts BILL.]

NAN: Wait—

BILL: I'm moving my things into Barbara's room.

[As NAN follows BILL to their house, GUS and DARCY hug each other with a hesitant joy. Lights on GUS and DARCY fade. BILL stands a short distance away from NAN.]

NAN: Maybe *I* should apologize. *(Beat.)* I'm calling Barbara now.

[BILL looks at her as if the whole thing's too late and then exits. As she awaits for Barbara to respond to her TTY call, lights on NAN fade.

Lights open on ALL standing where they were in the beginning of the play. Before speaking, each CHARACTER will speak to the audience, and then drift away.]

VICKI: For a long time after that I didn't see Gus. I thought about him day and night, and the ghost of him that haunted me faded into dust. I decided to go to Lansel State University and study for a Master's in English literature. There, I met Lance, who's hearing. I'm still amazed at how quickly he'd picked up on signs, and how smart and challenging he really is—we've had some wonderful debates. (*Beat.*) Sometimes Lance feels lost in the banter of my deaf friends, but he says that all good things take time.

GUS: For the longest time I didn't see Vicki. One morning she and her new husband Lance came into my office to discuss mortgage possibilities, and I was so happy to see her so radiant with Lance. (*Beat.*) As for Bill and Nan, I try not to feel bad over what happened, but even Darcy tells me that she understands what *real* friendship is. (*Beat.*) I still don't consider Nan to be a good friend. Every time I see her, she asks about my job and then leaves me alone. (*Beat.*) Bill wants to set up a new club in which we all could try a new sport every month. If that happens, we'll accept checks only.

BILL: For the longest time I didn't visit Gus at the bank. I read in the *Lansel Gazette* that he was promoted again after he caught two of his co-workers embezzling his bank. That was big news for a while, and I felt so proud of him. (*Beat.*) Finally, one day I walked into his new office and we just . . . hugged each other. It was a strange, wonderful feeling. (*Beat.*) Some nights I dream about Vicki sleeping in my arms, and then when I wake up, I find Nan shivering. (*Beat.*) Nan and I are still married. Married? Why? Guess it's an old habit. (*Beat.*) But Barbara still refuses to come home.

DARCY: For a long time after that, I didn't see either Bill or Nan. I thought about them, and I really missed Nan. I'd drive by the deaf school and then all the memories would come back like a waterfall. (*Beat.*) Gus and I still go out to deaf events, but we've become more choosy about who our friends are. Seems better that way. (*Beat.*) Even then, I was giving Bill and Nan fake smiles across the room at deaf events until one day I found myself standing opposite Nan. She looked so alone. She wept out there in the open, and *I* held her.

NAN: For the longest time, I didn't see Vicki. (*Sighs.*) One day on the street I saw her with her husband. He was a very good-looking man, and he turned around when Vicki said something to him. I didn't catch what she said, but I caught his look. I knew exactly what she'd said. (*Beat.*) I never start rumors—well, I *repeated* them, that's all. (*Beat.*) I feel everyone's eyes on me everywhere I go. I have to force myself to show up at deaf events in town. I feel their eyes burning right into my soul. I know I have to earn their trust again. (*Beat.*) Without trust, I'm nothing.

[Lights dim as ALL trade places with each other. They look at each other with averted eyes. Lights bounce from one character to the next.]

VICKI: Rumors have no name tag.

GUS: Tiny little lies are born every day.

BILL: Rumors seem to outlive us all.

DARCY: Pain is an open secret.

NAN: Rumors are like a big onion—when peeled, all layers, all tears, and nothing there.

[Lights fade to BLACKOUT.]

About the Author

Raymond Luczak is the author and editor of ten books, including *Assembly Required: Notes from a Deaf Gay Life*, *St. Michael's Fall: Poems*, and *Eyes of Desire 2: A Deaf GLBT Reader*. His novel *Men with Their Hands* won first place in the Project: QueerLit 2006 Contest. His work has appeared in over ten anthologies and many periodicals. Sixteen of his stage plays have been performed in three countries. Luczak has directed the full-length documentaries *Guy Wonder: Stories & Artwork* and *Nathie: No Hand-Me-Downs*, as well as his debut feature film *Ghosted*. He has collaborated with the renowned storyteller Manny Hernandez on his first two DVDs: *Manny ASL: Stories in American Sign Language* and *Manny: ASL for a Better Life*. He resides in Minneapolis, Minnesota. His web site is www.raymondluczak.com